STRIPPED

A MEMOIR

Lucian S.

Bibliografische Informationen der Deutschen Nationalbibliothek:
Die Deutsche Nationalbibliothek verzeichnet diese Publikation in
der Deutschen Nationalbibliografie; detaillierte bibliografische
Daten sind im Internet über dnb.dnb.de abrufbar.

Die automatisierte Analyse des Werkes, um daraus Informationen
insbesondere über Muster, Trends und Korrelationen gemäß §44b
UrhG („Text und Data Mining") zu gewinnen, ist untersagt.
© 2024, Lucian S.
Publisher: BoD · Books on Demand GmbH, In de Tarpen 42,
22848 Norderstedt, bod@bod.de
Print: Libri Plureos GmbH, Friedensallee 273, 22763 Hamburg

Coverbild: Younesse/pexels.com
Covergestaltung: Lucian S.

ISBN: 978-3-7597-5273-4

الكَرَاهِيَّة، لَا يُمْكِنْ أَنْ تَحْبَلْ، وَ لَا أَنْ تَلِدْ

نِزَار قَبَّانِي

Hatred can neither conceive nor give birth.

Nizar Qabbani

Prologue

If you can't see other than what light is showing you and you can't hear other than what voices announce to you, so dear, the truth is that you can't see or hear. The truth needs two people: one to say it and one to perceive it. In this book, there are many challenging events. Please do not continue if you are dependent on your present belief system and do not accept others or feel you cannot cope emotionally with what has happened and is happening in some people's lives. Please do not continue if you are an "I know it all" type of person or if your religion is worth killing for. I assure you that there's nothing for you in this book.

If you choose to continue, please remember that some of us are like ink, and others are like paper. If it were not for some of us to be dark, the white would be deaf, and if it were not for the whiteness of some of us, the blackness would be blind.

Whenever I thought about holding a pen and starting to write, I stopped myself in any way I could to forget about it because I knew that deep inside, I was not even ready to hear my thoughts—much less share them with others. Because, trust me, you may lose your mind trying to understand mine.

But here I am, starting another thing to do. Not for myself, but to make a difference or at least to inspire someone that life moves on, and the show must go on with or without us. It is time to tell the whole damn world that we exist, and we will simply be ourselves with our unique fingerprints.

You may wonder what you will see in a book titled *Stripped*. Is it about being physically nude? Are you going to see nude photos between pages?

Let's be honest: Sex sells!

But no, you will not ... It will be way more interesting. It is about being nude in a different way, with no secrets, no stories to hide behind, and no clothes or masks to put on because not one of us was born covered. The first thing they did to us was cover us with a piece of fabric, a name to carry till we die, and a life we must live whether we like it or not. I decided to strip myself of everything I was covered with. I felt like it was worth it to walk upon the earth with no name and no clothes to be covered with, to walk only with my storytelling of who I might be, while my body is the paper of this book, and my features are drawn with the ink of all these words.

I always did my best to save my privacy. I have never liked people to know what is going on in my life. Even the closest people to me knew nothing in detail. I always wanted to handle my issues, sadness, and struggles alone. As it was once said, "Don't let people know too much about you; if they know more, they will find many ways to hurt you." Sharing some of my stories with strangers is like walking nude for me. Then I remembered that we were all born with no cover on. It makes sense to me because if covering our bodies all the time is that important and is a central issue around the globe, then why were we all born naked?

At first, I was planning to start writing this book and hide behind the pronoun HE Instead of I. Two letters could give me a better chance to avoid trouble, but I wanted to play this with my own rules and with the one letter that describes me and all of us the most. It is time for me to run my own show.

So, let's be just you and me, just the two of us, during these pages. I am going to tell you a lot of my story. I will imagine that we have known each other for a long time while talking to you just like I am talking to someone very close to me, whom I can trust to listen to without judgment.

One.

As once said, "When you pay attention, everything is your teacher."

I paid attention to almost everything since I was a little kid. I came to this world with so many questions like "Who's God? How old is he? Why He, not She? Why do we even breathe, and why did I come to this world in this particular place and time?"

I was a child who struggled for years to read and write, while most of the kids my age did it way earlier than I did. Somehow, my brain was ahead of many at my age, as I always wanted to know things instead of learning what I was told to learn. As a result of that, kids and adults called me so many names, such as "stupid, disabled," and "crazy," Struggling with reading, I always felt less of myself as a child, but when I did learn how to read, I didn't stop, and I won't till the day I die. I still remember the first story I ever read. It was written by the Greek fabulist and storyteller Aesop. The story was about Zeus, who created humans carrying two bags. One is hanging in the front and is full of other people's shortfalls, and the other is hanging in the back, full of one's own shortfalls. This is why people can see the shortfalls of others and never see their own. This story made me, in one way or another, the person I am today. It made me always busy checking my back in the mirror, as I wanted to become a better version of myself. That made me busy enough to forget about checking the bag in the front. It made me blind to what other people might genuinely be and what they hid from me. Later on, all the names some people called me were replaced by the names *Al Tant* and *Al kharoof* (Faggot, sheep). A sheep because I have curly hair, and a faggot, because I was never someone who would make a fight, and that made me less than an ordinary boy in their eyes.

I used to hate school because, again, it was never the place to learn about what I wanted to know, it was to learn about what they wanted me to know. Just a few people had answers to my many questions since I was a child. One of them was my father. He used to drink a glass of Arak every night while having dinner. It was my favorite time because it was the time when my father would answer some of my questions and discuss almost anything with me. That was when I was between the ages of eight and fifteen. This was the school I loved the most, with one teacher and one class, where there were no forbidden questions. He taught me how to be the best version of myself. He taught me that God is not the punisher who waits for our mistakes, but that God is true peace and love, love in all kinds and ways, is inside every one of us, and he is our brain that tells us the bad and the good. My father has those gorgeous blue-grey eyes, like the earth's color from out of space, that make you feel like he has the wisdom of it; if the earth could speak, it would talk just like him. He taught me that there is no limit to learning. Every time we learn about something, we ask for more and still have much to know. Unlimited knowledge is something unreachable.

My dad was born and raised in a small village. The closest school to his modest house was a two-hour drive. He used to go there every single day, no matter what the weather was or how he had to get there, by bus or even walking. He knew exactly what he wanted, and he achieved it. He became an engineer and the first person in that area to earn a degree above middle school. He made it from totally nothing. I am so proud to have an amazing father like him.

My definition of female beauty was always a lady with long black hair, hazel eyes, bronze skin tone, long beautiful legs, with a gorgeous body, and she had to be a smoker.

My mom completely inspired my definition of female beauty. For me, "The beauty of the whole universe has been shortened in Mama." She kind of grew up as an orphan and was raised by her lovely aunt after her dad had left because he was busy with his new wife and new children. They always told her that her mom had passed away when my mom was two years old. She had lived with this idea until her early twenties when she was on a trip to Lebanon with her friends. She accidentally met her mom in a restaurant in Beirut.

My grandmother was sitting there with her friend at a table next to the door, having her coffee, when a group of girls entered through that wooden door with a brass bell above it. She had no idea that the tinkle of that brass bell would be the start of being a mom again. When she saw them, her heart started beating so fast; she told her friend, "How life is so unfair. I am sure that my daughter is somewhere looking gorgeous, just like those beautiful young ladies and just like her own mom." Then they laughed about how much my grandma loved how she looked.

My mom has a unique name that I have never heard of before, nor have I even heard of someone else having it. After around fifteen minutes, one of my mom's friends said her name. At that moment, a bell tinkled fast and loud inside my grandma's heart like a church bell on a Sunday. Without hesitating, she stood up, walked to my mom's table, looked deeply into my mom's eyes, and asked, "Is that your name?" My mom kept silent for a few seconds before answering, so she asked again, "Is that your name?" My mom replied, "Yes, it is! Why?" My grandma asked, "Is your second name ......?" - "Yes, do we know each other?" At that point, my grandma fell on her knees, started crying, and hugged her like in a scene in an Italian opera. She told her she was her mother with a shivery, gravelly voice that kept my mom from questioning whether she heard the same thing. And then my mom said, even in a more shivery voice: "But my mom passed away when I was two years old! It is not possible!" During the next couple of hours, my mom heard the whole truth about the lie she had been living every single day of her past life. She heard about how her mom ran away in the middle of the night because of her husband, who used to beat her just for being an attractive woman he wanted to keep only for himself and didn't allow her even to leave the house. Sadly, my grandma had to put herself first and fled to Lebanon. The price she paid for being free was to leave her daughter to live as a motherless girl. But I believe this is what God is for. He takes care of each one of us in his own way.

I have this unique relationship with my mom. She is not only my sweet mom but also my friend, and I try my best to be a mom and a dad for her, in addition to being a good son. She taught me not only about love but also about giving and caring. She mentioned not only how much it may hurt to give or care but also how many people deserve our care and will return it to us in many ways.

Mom and Dad helped me find out how to achieve my dreams even out of nothing. They showed me how much even a simple smile to a stranger could make his day. They taught me whom I must love: "Fall in love with someone strong because this person might be the only army you need."

Two.

I was raised in a middle-class family that offered almost everything to me except inner peace of mind. It took me quite a while to figure out that I had to find and achieve this on my own. At first, I couldn't find it because I was not honest with myself or supportive enough.

Every time I felt attracted to a guy, I ignored my feelings and him, not because I was ashamed of who I was but because I could be rejected. Even if he were gay, he would hide it and bully me for something within himself that he was fighting against. This is how many people in the LGBTQ community live their lives. They have sex with random people, and in public, they are ladies and gentlemen. They may not have the knowledge that they could be both homosexuals and ladies or gentlemen at the same time.

This is something that made me different from the start. I couldn't let some rules, created by people whose names no one knows or if they even existed or not, control how I had to live my life under the power and the name of conventionality or even religion. I often say: "As long as I am not hurting anybody, including myself, it is not your damn business whom I like to share my bed with."

An African proverb says, "When there is no enemy within, the enemies outside can't hurt you." This is how I became my best friend: deep inside, I knew that I was choosing the hard road and needed trustworthy company.

I knew I would only have what I wanted if I did what the rest were doing. I couldn't do that because I couldn't be anything but myself.

I started to see the world through a 15-inch screen. I began to search on the internet for something like what I was going through. That was the first time I saw how closed-minded the Arabic-speaking world is. I found out that in Arabic, we have a name. That name was close enough to be the name of the plague (Shaz). When I searched about the same in English, I found the word "Gay." I began to feel happy, normal and accepted as a human being. Then, I started the journey to see myself as a normal 16-year-old guy. During the first month of being even a bit open about who I was, I lost a few of my close friends. I also lost my favorite uncle at that time. He told his wife to tell me at the door that I was not allowed to enter their place again and that I was dead for the whole family. That caused me much pain, but I somehow sucked it up and moved on.

I met a lot of both bad and good people online. I met the people who make you feel like they hadn't heard about something called "Hi" or "Hello." All they used to do at first was ask for nude photos or about your role in bed. I couldn't accept that kind of person. I always admired the intellectual, polite, "classy" type of man. I met some of those men online and am still friends with some of them. My only problem was that all the guys I liked lived more than 2,000 miles away.

Eventually, at 16, I decided to leave school and study at home because I couldn't handle bullying. Boys at school used to bully me since I was eight years old. I went through eight years and a half of bullying, not because of anything except that I was different from them. On the other hand, girls used to like me at school, and all of them were my friends. That was one of the reasons boys hated me at school even more. I was always a straight-looking and acting guy, well dressed and always in love with perfumes. That kind of difference I was talking about before. I am a skinny guy with broad shoulders and 1.80 meters in height. I was not like this back then. I was a thin, short boy with curly hair, messy eyelashes, and sad eyes. Every boy at that school was bigger and taller than me, so they quickly showed off their strength by bullying me. They used to wait for me in front of the school's gate after we finished classes. I had a different plan and an inner map every day to leave school without letting them see me. They beat me a few times before I learned where my strength lay. It was on my tongue. I was blessed with a tongue that I knew exactly how to use and when. That strong muscle I have was my weapon because, without it, I could only live a life controlled by a society that creates sons who believe that if they don't make trouble or beat other boys, they would never be real men.

It all started when I woke up one morning and wanted to wear my red shoes. This was not allowed at school. They had to be black. Just then, I decided that I was not going there again. I left the house for a whole week at the same time I used to leave every day. After school, I used to walk to the beach and sit until I had to be home. I told my mom the next week that I didn't want to go to school that day, and she asked, "Are you okay? Is it all good at school?" I said: "Yes, kind of, but I don't want to go today." She said OKAY. An hour later, someone from school called our house and wanted to talk to my mom to ask her why I missed a few days at school. When they asked her that, she looked at me and said: "His dad and I don't want him to go there anymore. He will study at home because your school is not a school we want our kid to be in."

At that point, I knew that my mom and dad felt I was unhappy there from the first day of that semester, but they needed some confirmation. They felt that I was going through a challenging difficulty and that I wanted to handle it on my own. I did take it on my own—by leaving a place where bullies surrounded me, and I am still glad that I did.

Three.

It is March 2015 at four in the morning, and the power is off. Under the light of a candle, I am trying to write about the next period I went through. Candles are nice and romantic, but only when you know you have power. It is hard for me to write about the period that will come next because this was the experience that didn't kill me but made me stronger. Yes, it didn't kill me and made me stronger, but it hurt me badly.

I started to have gay friends from around here. I met some online and some others through mutual friends. I thought that, finally, I was going to fit in somewhere. But no, I was mistaken. Or maybe I was not lucky enough to meet the good version of gay people here because, at that time, I learned what kind of gay people this society had formed. Let me tell you something about gay people here, or at least those I knew who were out of the closet. They are the biggest enemies of one another —by stealing each other's boyfriends or at least "Doing" them or calling the other one's parents to tell them about the sexuality of their sons. These sons would often be kicked out of their own homes. And finally, they use some people they know to get each other arrested.

I had plenty of experiences like that because of people I thought would have the same dreams as humans or even as citizens. Because of people I thought would look after each other. Trust me, there were moments when I missed the bullies back at school.

I always hated the word "victim" and promised never to be one or act like one. But, as some people say and believe, some things in our lives are meant to happen. I knew what it meant to be one of those people and how it felt. I guess it made me a little bit wiser as a human being and gave me experience.

There is this coffee shop where gay guys used to hang out. I used to go there with the gay friends I had back then almost every day. I remember it was a rainy, cold evening when we went there one day. We sat at our usual table. Some of us were smoking shisha. The place was full of gay people who all knew each other. After sitting there for around twenty minutes, a handsome, tall man entered the door. All the guys in this coffee shop turned quiet for a few seconds because of the handsome stranger drenched in the rain. He was new to that place, and everyone was trying his best to be the first to talk to him. Most of the guys at my table were trying, smiling at him, and winking flirtatiously like the others. All of this was brand new to me. I felt so embarrassed and confused. I did not know if I should stay inside that place or leave. I left ten minutes later because I was so uncomfortable around people acting like sex machines.

The next day, I knew that the table that had won the contest to conquer the hot stranger was my friend's. It turned out that he sat with them after I left, and of course, nobody at the other tables was happy about that, especially one effeminate guy in his middle thirties. He used to get upset and aggressive if someone spoke to him as a man. He thought of it as an insult. He was known to be high on drugs all the time. Everyone considered him a horrible person. His primary sources of income were prostitution or pimping, and he was a drug dealer from time to time, so he knew many troubled people and had much dirty money.

I stopped going to the coffee shop for a few days because I had to study. After a while, I felt bored and convinced myself how useless it was to feel so embarrassed for something I did not even do. I called one of my friends and asked him to meet me at the coffee shop.

I went there to see that handsome stranger sitting at our table. I said "Hi" to everyone and ordered my regular sweet coffee. I moved a chair and sat next to one of my friends. The handsome stranger also moved his chair and put it next to mine. He reached out his hand and said: "Hi, I am Aman, and I heard a lot about you." I replied: "My pleasure. I'm Lucian." Then he said in a low voice: "Actually, I know nothing about you because no one wanted to tell me anything. But here I am, and I want to get to know you more if you allow it." We chatted for almost an hour about all sorts of things. I asked him with all the confidence I could manage during our conversation: "Why me? Look around! Everybody is craving even to talk to you." — "First, because you are not," he replied, "and second, I love guys who play hard to get." And that was something I was not intentionally doing at all. For me, the sexiest body part is the mind. Also, I am the kind of person who is committed to the credo, "If anyone can have it, I don't want it." I also wanted to get to know him because he was so polite and confident, and he was the first guy who flirted with me in real life without living 2,000 miles away through a 15-inch screen.

We exchanged cell phone numbers and decided to meet again somewhere else — away from that place. We left together, and he waited until I took a cab. While sitting in the cab on my way home, one of my friends called me to tell me one of the most horrible, terrifying things to hear for a teenage gay guy like me. He told me that the effeminate guy who used to call himself "Afaf" had come to their table after I had left with Aman and started yelling and threatening them. He demanded to give him my land phone number. One of my closest friends - that's what I thought he was - asked Afaf if he could have a word and took him away from the table. He asked Afaf for money in return for handing over my number. They struck that deal, and after that, my friends saw Afaf shouting and screaming on his cell phone, telling one of my parents that "Your son is a damn faggot, and he just left with a hot guy to get fucked."

When my friend and I ended that call, I cried and was utterly terrified. I didn't know what to do or what to say. Did I have to go back? Did I have to go home? Which of my parents answered him? What would my parents do to me? Would they be disappointed in me? Why hadn't one of my parents called me yet? Who would I call right now? Sadly, I had no one to call for advice or to help me calm down.

I took a deep breath and started to think about what I was going to do, what I was going to say. Then it hit me that I had to get home as quickly as possible because Afaf had told my parents that I just went out with some guy to have sex. If I came home soon, they would know he was a damn liar. I thought through everything during these minutes and decided that if they asked me about my sexuality, I would not lie about who I am —no matter the price. I was a gay guy who hadn't received even a kiss from another guy yet.

I respected myself for who I was, not because of any experience with another guy.

When I entered the house, it was unnaturally quiet. Then I heard my mom from the kitchen asking: "Habibi, is that you?" I waited a few seconds until I could answer her. She asked me to give her a hand with something. I went to the kitchen, and when I looked at my mom's face, I realized that she had something to say to me. She noticed the fear in my eyes and asked me if everything was okay. "Yes, kind of," I said. "Look, my prince, someone called us and tried to tell me some stuff about you. I didn't let him finish and told him I would call the police if he called again. I don't want to ask you about anything, but I will ask you to stop talking to anyone at that coffee place. None of them is good enough for you. Change your cellphone number tomorrow. I don't want any of them to bother you or get in touch with you. I trust you and am sure you know what's best for you."

I knew deep inside that my mom was right. These people were not good for me. The next morning, I got a new cellphone number. On my way to the store, I received a text message: Afaf had paid more money to get the land phone numbers of my friends at school. He had called their parents one by one to tell them that I was a "faggot." Not one of them would talk to me anymore. After I finished reading this text, I wished only to be invisible. I remember sitting on the sidewalk, feeling so lonely, thinking of nothing. Then I broke the SIM card of my old cellphone number.

I stayed inside my room for a couple of days doing nothing except crying and listening to music before I started to think: Why am I here crying because of people who want me to cry and feel hurt? Why am I giving them exactly what they want that easily? I am so much fucking stronger and smarter than this.

That was the first thing that made me develop trust issues. I am getting my revenge now from that thing called Afaf by telling his story and using "He." Trust me, to my mind, it would drive him crazy, although I don't think he is able to read Arabic, much less English.

Karma does its job in so many ways. The friend who sold my land phone number and my friends' numbers to Afaf lives in Turkey now, using drugs. And I have never heard anything from that handsome stranger who called himself Aman.

Four.

Music has had an enormous influence on me ever since that time. I went through so much depression, but the next few months were my first time dealing with such a gut punch of negative feelings. I remember how many times I thought about ending my own life at that time. Music always used to get me out of that dark zone.

Sometimes, all we need to do is listen to the right song. I have always been a fan of music that makes you feel better and stronger. Sometimes, I needed to hear sad music with sad lyrics because it made me feel like it was expressing everything I went through—even more since I had no one to talk to about it. It is like saying out loud what's going on in your mind that you can't say for yourself.

I spent most of my time alone in my bedroom studying, listening to music, and overthinking everything. Overthinking took me to dark places so many times. I felt alone and like everybody would be embarrassed even to say "Hi" to me. When I left the house, I was convinced that everyone was staring at me, knowing what was happening inside my head and judging me. It was all because of overthinking about something. I acted like it would not hurt, but it hurt very much.

My parents started to control my life more and more. They made many things forbidden for me, but I've always been the kind who rebels against rules — as long as I am not hurting anyone, including myself.

Jail is any place you cannot leave. I know exactly what that means because I experienced it every moment in my homeland. I felt the same when I was stuck at the house because it was something my parents wanted me to do. Then I learned how to say "No"— to really mean it and act accordingly.

I have just one brother who is older than me by a few years. He was always the tough, masculine guy who embodied the image of straight society. My brother and I never had a close relationship, even when we shared the same room as kids. He attended a different school and hung out with other friends. I always felt like my brother was embarrassed once his friends knew that I was his only brother. This seemed to be all because I was not a troublemaker, and my friends were mostly girls. My brother is such a sweetheart inside, and I don't blame him because you must always be tough to survive in an environment like here. He kicked many boys' asses back at school just because they bullied me. It all changed when we grew up. People do change when they get older, don't they?

On June 21st of the same year, it was my birthday. I did nothing special like every other birthday except think and dream of where I would possibly be next year on this exact date. The next day, I argued with my brother about why I was keeping my hair long. Wearing your hair like this around here is unusual if you look like a straight, masculine guy. The argument grew because I was done hearing from people what I had to do and what not. I fired back, which is unacceptable to come from a younger brother. I couldn't help but use my sharp tongue, my weapon, to fight mean people or defend myself. And my brother was really mean to me that day. I remember when he felt he couldn't answer me anymore. He told me something that makes me feel so hurt even today. "Look fag," he said, "Don't ever say that I am your brother because I am not, not anymore. You are an embarrassment. You are dead to me." My parents were there during the whole argument. They said nothing when he told me that. It was the first time I left the house crying because I felt like my parents agreed with him when they chose to stay silent.

I left the house and started to walk without knowing where to go. I walked to whatever place my feet were carrying me. I felt nothing new at that time. I was feeling so alone. People on the streets looked at me, wondering why I was crying, but no one bothered to ask.

After a couple of hours, my feet took me back to our apartment building. I remember sitting on the sidewalk. I was staring at the window of my room, thinking of all my feelings, thoughts, and dreams since childhood. There was so much to remember. When I came back home, I talked to nobody there. The next day, I began to stop fighting my teenage hormones. Instead, I just ignored everybody around me, including my parents.

Is it okay to live a life others don't understand?

I kept this up for around a week. Then I decided to find another place where I could find gay people around here, and I found it quickly. I wanted to be a brand-new person and a stronger version of myself. I acted like I didn't care about anything, like I had nothing to lose. This was, of course, not true. We don't appreciate what we have until it is sadly gone. I was doing everything my hormones were driving me to do to ignore my loneliness. Here I am, blaming my hormones as a teenager instead of the whole society for what happened to me next. How sweet of me!

I made new friendships with new gay guys from around here. I started to hang out with more and more people day after day. I became friends with practically everyone gay in my city. I didn't see much difference between them and the people at the gay coffee place in the past. Most of them had the same attitude and even the same lifestyle. Sex meant almost everything to them.

I became more and more popular in a short time. I was so good at playing the character I was playing around them. But I also remember being rude to rude guys who used to bully others to show everyone that I was not the one to mess with. Deep inside, it was all about seeing the old me bullied by mean people—like those poor guys. The old me had no one to protect him—but those others would have me around them.

I learned more and more during that time about gay life and how they got to know each other. They invented their own language to talk to one another. They use it when they don't want anyone around to understand them. They may use it to talk about a hot guy sitting next to them or maybe about money and escort business, which is prevalent in their environment. Some of them became escorts to survive after leaving their parent's house. Others did it just for fun. They love sex and an expensive lifestyle, so being an escort for them was like a dream job.

After a while, their language became not a secret anymore and was known to many who were not gays, thanks to the gay guys who would do anything to make out with straight ones. Those straight guys would brag for hours about how many girls begged them to have sex, and a few hours later, they would be bottoms in bed with gay guys who wear wigs. The following day, they will return to being the tough guys and will bully every gay that they see on the streets.

I had my own experience with this kind of guy, but it differed from the one other gays went through.

It was a cold winter night when I walked with one of my friends. The streets were empty, and just a few cars were passing by. I remember seeing two guys standing in a corner. It was dark over there. The only thing I could see was the glow of two cigarettes. When those guys saw us, they began to follow us slowly. While walking, I laughed with my friend but feared them deep inside. I couldn't show my fear because I knew that they were similar to animals—they smelled fear. My friend was wearing some makeup, so they could tell we were gay. They kept following us for more than thirty minutes and were coming closer. They started to throw some words: "We are horny." and "We want to fuck." That made me even more scared because they looked like troubled people. Ten minutes later, they stood before us and asked us to talk—I was shaking. Again, they asked us for sex. "We know a place we can go to," one of them said. I remember that one was around 1.95 cm tall, and the other was shorter than me. The short guy was the one who did all the talking with all his rudeness. He made me feel like it was an order to have sex with them, and we had to do it immediately. I hid my hands inside my pockets so they wouldn't see them shaking. My brain worked so fast; unfortunately, I used my sharp tongue when he finished talking. I told him to grab a chair and stand on it so I could see him first—next time he wants to speak to us. We left and walked as fast as we could, looking behind us every few minutes to see if they were still following us. After a while, in the middle of the empty street, I could hear someone running toward us from behind. I was terrified enough not to look behind me. I felt something sharp and cold entering my back. One of the guys had stabbed me between my shoulders with a razor, and both ran away like rats.

I remember my friend screaming while putting his hand on my back and pressing hard on the wound. I felt no pain. All I was feeling was being lost. I couldn't understand what was happening until I saw my friend's hands covered with blood, covered with my blood; I saw his hands while he was screaming for a cab to take us to the hospital. He hugged me and told me that everything was going to be okay. The last thing I could remember from that night was the smell of my blood, which made me unconscious. After a few hours, I woke up in the hospital, full of pain. The razor had entered my body close to the spine. There were two wounds on my back, which needed seven stitches each. No one told me how deep the wounds were, but I had to keep the stitches for around three weeks and wasn't allowed by the doctors to leave bed or move.

The two scars are still on my back, and every time I see them in the mirror, I ask myself if it would have been wiser to do what they wanted—to avoid what happened that night. But at the same time, I knew I would do exactly what I did again, and my reaction would be the same.

Of course, my parents never knew the truth about what happened that day. I was lucky that I didn't get killed during that cold night or that they didn't attack my face with that razor. If I had been mature enough then, all I would have had to do was stay away from that lifestyle and keep my life only inside the fifteen-inch screen of my computer until I had the chance to leave. I didn't because I needed to be closer to something and wanted to know exactly what it was. I had many questions and thought I could find the answers somewhere in that lifestyle. So I returned to that life the day the doctors removed the stitches. I started to hang out again with the same friends every day. The fear was something attached to me all the time. I feared going through anything I had gone through before, but I was acting like the guy who had the thickest skin ever. I lived daily without thinking about the future and trying to forget the past.

I remember the first gay party I attended. It was something unforgettable for me as a gay teenager. It was a birthday party, and many guys were in that big beach house the host had rented. Some of them were shirtless, and others were wearing women's clothes. The only thing that was in common between all of them was that they were drunk. There was a locked room upstairs where they put all the stuff they didn't want to lose, and only a couple of guys had the keys. I went up there with one of my friends to store our wallets and cell phones. Then we went downstairs to enjoy our first gay party. The music was so loud that we couldn't even talk. There was a DJ who played the most horrible Arabic songs I have ever heard, songs for belly dancing. It became like a competition for them to see who was dancing better.

I was sitting alone the whole time, watching drunk people dancing—asking myself If I belonged to this community. A few guys approached me and asked me to join them, but I refused politely. I didn't drink at that party because I was under eighteen, but I was not the only one underage there. Many guys my age were smoking weed and drinking. One hour later, some drunk, shirtless guy approached me, and without even saying one word, he hit me with the beer can he was holding. I was shocked for a second, but then I pushed him away. A few guys came between us to stop any fight that could happen. I have never believed in violence. This is why I did not even try to hit him back, but trust me, loud music saved him that night because if there hadn't been loud music over there, I could have said things to him that might have made him cry in front of everyone at that party. He came after ten minutes to apologize. He said he drank a lot and didn't know what he was thinking. One of the guys who asked me to dance was his ex-boyfriend, who was still in love with him. I guess I was somehow in the wrong place at the wrong time.

After a while, we heard shouting upstairs that drowned out the loud music. The DJ turned the music off, and we started rushing upstairs to find out what was happening. No one went upstairs who also didn't start to yell. I saw all of the party people standing in front of the locked room door, where everybody kept their stuff. Everyone was blaming or accusing. The door was broken, and most of the things were gone. Someone had stolen everything he could carry without anyone noticing him. I said before: I was in the wrong place at the wrong time. My wallet and my cellphone were stolen too. I was so mad and upset that night, but when I remember it now, I laugh about what an unlucky day it has been. It was a fun, easy night to remember compared to what had happened to me the next day.

Five.

I am trying to write about the next period I went through. It was the period that changed everything for me. It changed my life, personality, appearance, and how I saw everything around me. Even now, I have nightmares occasionally about that time. Even mentioning it is so damn hard for me, so what about remembering it with specific details and sharing it with you? Some say: "Talk about things that make you feel bad; it will make you feel better." No, it doesn't. It is all about who you talk about it with. I had no one to talk to except myself. It took me quite a while to almost heal myself, but I am proud that I could do that with no one's help or support.

"Go inside of it, and you will go missing. Leave out of it, and you will be reborn again." This saying is somewhat mysterious but has a very concrete meaning. I went inside of it, left out of it, and was reborn again a few months after my eighteenth birthday. I spent three days inside, and it took me more than three years to recover in some ways.

It was like any regular evening when I went to the internet cafe. I used to talk with people from around the world who spoke English. They used to find me on gay social websites. I got a few messages that day. One of the messages came from a guy who seemed friendly, polite, and educated. I replied to him, and we started to chat the same evening. For a lot of those men, I was the brave young gay guy who posted his clear-face pictures on gay websites while he lived in the Middle East.

He told me he was French and lived and worked as an oil engineer in Dubai. He was visiting some friends in Lebanon. We chatted for more than three hours that night. I eventually gave him my cellphone number. He called me immediately to hear my voice. He had this French-English accent and used many French words. I liked him. I admire people who speak several languages. We talked on the phone for a few hours to get to know each other better. He said: "If we were closer, I would do anything to take you out on a date." I had never done that before but kept it to myself and didn't share it with him.

We ended our call at midnight and decided to stay in touch until we found a way to meet. He had mentioned a few times during that call that he would be crazy enough to travel from one country to another just to have dinner with a guy like me. I was flattered, but I couldn't imagine he would do it. I thought this was just one of these internet talks, but actually, he did it.

He booked a flight to my city immediately after we had ended that call. I woke up the following day to find his message that he couldn't stop himself from coming. "I didn't want to waste the chance to take you out for dinner," he wrote. He told me where he was staying and when he would wait for me to have dinner in the five-star hotel he was staying in. I was happy that I would have my first date with a guy like him. I wore my best clothes and my favorite perfume. I knew it would be a day that would stay in my memory for a long time. This would be true, but not in the category of memories I thought of.

When I entered that fancy hotel, I went to the reception desk and asked about the dinner reservation. The woman at the front desk looked at me and asked for my ID. "Maybe she wants to check if I am over eighteen," I thought, so I gave it to her. She returned it after a couple of minutes. I went to my table to find a classy man waiting for me. We had a nice dinner. We talked about many things, but gay life and the gay scene were always at the center of the conversation. He also spoke about how hard it is to be in a relationship with a guy and how we always do our best to hide our love instead of showing it. He talked nonstop about his previous love affairs the moment he knew he was my first date ever. After a few hours, he told me he had to leave early to catch his flight to Paris from Beirut. "We will stay in touch," we promised each other.

After that, I felt above the clouds, but this feeling didn't stay much longer. Two days later, at nine in the morning, I was still up because I always liked studying the whole night and sleeping in the morning. After breakfast with my mom, I went to my room to sleep. Suddenly, the doorbell rang. I was lying on my bed, trying to fall asleep. The moment I heard the bell, I sat up. My hands were shaking. I just felt unsafe for no reason. My mom opened the door.

I heard the voices of three different men. They asked about me, saying my full name. Now I started panicking for real. I left my bed and sneaked to the door of my room, trying to grasp what was happening. I heard my mom saying: "There must be a mistake. It can't be him. Are you sure of the name? Maybe there is someone else with the same name?" My mom called my dad, asking him to come home immediately. "It is an emergency," she said. When I heard that, my knees did not carry me anymore. I sat behind the door of my room, trying to listen more about what was going on. When my dad came, the men introduced themselves as agents from some branch of the police. They all started whispering. My dad repeated my mom's words: "There must be a mistake. It can't be him." After thirty minutes, they left, and the silence took over—no one was saying a word. I returned to bed and acted like I was asleep the whole time. When I woke up, everything seemed normal except for the awkward silence.

My parents called me and said, "Sit down, son." Then my dad asked, "Where have you been two days ago for dinner?" "I had dinner with a friend. Why?" "Who is this friend, and where is he from?" "We met online, and he is French. He was here in town, so we had dinner together." "Is that all? It is not all. Three men came this morning asking about you. They want to investigate you."

I sighed and said, "And why is all that?" "Are you trying to blow up your life?" my father asked me. "Are you trying to ruin your future?" "What have I done to ruin my life? A guy around my age, whom I met online and befriended, was in town, and I met him for dinner. What's wrong with that?" My father shook his head and said: "He is not a French guy. He is Saudi, and he is not around your age. He is more than twenty years older. And what did he say he is working?" I said: "It can't be. He does not sound like a Saudi. I am not that stupid. He works as an oil engineer in Dubai." "Sadly, he made you look way too stupid. He is an army officer from Saudi Arabia who lied to you about every detail and took advantage of you being young, and I don't know what else. The police believe that he is a damn spy", my father said, and he looked away to avoid any eye contact. "Did you have sex with him? Be honest with me so we can protect you." "What? Hell no! I didn't have sex with him. We were at the restaurant the whole time. We did not leave the table or even take a walk." "But the agents claim they have a video of you having sex with him in his hotel room. They even asked me if I wanted to see it." I said: "Wow, this is something! Call them and tell them you

want to see the video of your son with that man so you can see what manipulative liars they are. This video can't exist because nothing ever happened."
"Their problem is not if you had sex with him or not. They do not care. They say you are young, and young people sometimes do stupid things. What they want to know is what sort of topics you both talked about together." I said: "If he might be a danger to my country, I can bring him back here so they can investigate him themselves instead of trying to manipulate me and play those mind games with me and my parents." "It is all settled now with them. Just go back to your room and focus on your study." I was scared but relieved at the same time. I thought it would be the end of it. But, of course, it wasn't.

The next day, I woke up, showered, and dried my hair. When my mom saw me, she said: "You do not have enough of this long hair? You better cut it short to avoid getting attention from people for a while." And I said: "Yeah, right. How long my hair is does not say anything bad or good about who I am. I don't care about what people say and what not—around here. People will talk bad and good no matter what."

Later, the phone rang, so I answered. There was a man on the line asking about me. When he realized that it was me speaking, he started to pepper me with questions. I asked him politely who he was. He was an investigator from another branch of the police. He ordered me to come to the station for a few questions and hung up. At that moment, my mom approached me and asked: "Why have you turned pale? Who was talking on the phone?"

At that moment, all I wished was the ground would open and suck me to nowhere and never return because I had no idea what to answer my mom or what I should do. But I pulled myself together and tried to process this call. I responded to my mom: "It is another investigator from another police branch who wants me to come over this afternoon for a few questions." My mom started panicking and shouting, "They won't leave you alone till they drive you and us crazy. Oh my God, this will end with a disaster!"

I went to my room, closed the door, and started crying. I believed everything my mom had said before. She came to my door, knocked, and entered, trying to calm me down and telling me they would be with me all the way, no matter what. "Nothing is going to hurt you." She promised.

After that, I stood up, went to the bathroom, locked the door, took the scissors, cut all my curls and shaved my head. In that mirror, I was staring at nothing but an ill boy with watery eyes. It is pretty painful to remember this because it is damn hard to see the people who love you the most, seeing you hurt so badly and knowing they can't do anything to stop the pain and the harm or even ease them.

Six.

In the afternoon, I went to the station for questioning. There was just an empty, dark, dull feeling. Deep inside, I knew I had to prepare for the worst and stay calm. At the gate, they took my ID, cell phone, and everything I carried with me. I had to wait in a big office for the questioning. No one was talking to me. People were passing the office, looking at me, and then the whispering would start—they wanted to break people with some mind games. For almost a week, the same shit happened over and over again. They used to keep me from eight in the morning till lunchtime. Then I had to go back there in the afternoon till eleven at night. Those hours, counted minute after minute, felt like years for me, like miserable years.

On the last day, I was full of anger and disrespect. I left that office, knocked on the officer's door, entered, and asked: "Hello, sir. Can I know why I have been waiting all those hours for a few days in a row just for a few questions? I feel like I am a criminal. What have I done to be here and to go through all these mind games?" He said: "It is okay. We'll be ready for you in a bit." After ten minutes, I left his office and was called to the investigation room. More than six people were in that room, but only one was asking the questions. The others were staring at me like some human lie detectors. Now, the questioning began, "How do you know him? How did you both meet, and where? What did you both talk about? Did he ask you suspicious questions about specific places? Does he know anyone here? Did he meet anyone other than you?"

After they finished the interrogation, they asked me about my Email-address, where I used to chat with him. I gave it to them. Then, they asked for the password. I also had to give it to them. There was no other option for me. I was freaking out because it was my email account for my entire gay life. Now they could read every conversation I had with gay people worldwide, every detail of how I was myself as a young gay guy, all the photos and recording messages.

They finished with me around ten thirty at night. On my way home, I stopped at an internet café to clean up my messenger from the conversations and delete my main picture. I blocked everyone and deleted all my contacts. I was crying like a toddler who fell for the first time. I felt like I was falling so fast and deep in the ground. Something was sucking me away from the surface of this world I was so scared of, and I had no strength to face it, at least at that time.

I went home to see my mom, relieved that her son returned, but at the same time, I could see worries in her eyes. It turned out that early in the morning, another police branch had asked about me in the neighborhood. They left a note for me with an order to ask me a few questions. The first thing that came to my head was: "What the fuck have I done so the whole country is questioning me? Obviously, my first damn gay date was considered a national problem. What about the rest of the twenty-four million people? I am the worst among all of them now!"

My dad tried to use some contacts with people he knew to find a solution for the whole issue.

He found an old friend who knew the officer questioning me. My dad and I went to that station at nine in the morning. Our names were registered on the gate. We took the stairs to the fifth-floor office. My dad calmed me down and reminded me he would be with me. "I won't leave you alone—nothing bad will happen."

A bold officer sat in the room. Next to his desk was a small bed. He greeted my dad and asked us to have a seat. He asked my dad about their mutual friend. They started a small talk. Then he told my dad: "My apologies, but I must ask you to leave. I must be alone with your son for the questioning. It won't take more than fifteen minutes. You can wait for him at the gate. No worries at all. It is just something quick and simple. There is no way that we need to keep him here tonight. And even if we had to, I promise he will sleep here on this bed in my office. Your son is like my son, and he is in safe hands."

When my dad left and the office door closed, the officer opened some random drawers. He wanted to waste some time until my dad was farther downstairs. The officer walked toward me and asked me to stand up, so I did. Out of nowhere, he said, "Did you have any sexual intercourse with this man?" I answered: "No, I did not. Why is everyone asking me this question?" He walked faster toward me while saying: "You piece of shit *tanta* (faggot)," and kicked me between my legs so damn hard, hard enough to make me pass out. Later, he woke me up by pouring cold water on my head.

When I regained consciousness, I started crying nonstop and saying to him while trying to breathe, "What have I done to deserve all of this? I did nothing wrong. I am begging you to let me go. My dad is waiting for me outside in the cold and in the pouring rain. It is already dark. For how long was I out? You promised my dad that you would treat me like your own son. Please let me go, please." He laughed and said, "My son will never be a fag. I am doing your dad a favor and treating you better than my son because I would kill him if he were like you. People like you are no different from bad bacteria or fucking insects. It turns out you will stay in our hospitality after all, but guess what? Not here on this bed, downstairs under the ground. I am sure you will love it; it is also a five-star hotel like the one where you met this shitty man."

He wrote by hand for over an hour, filling a dozen papers with his words. It turned out that he was writing my confession—a confession I never made.

While writing, he looked at me loathsomely and said, "Who fucked the other? He fucked you, or you fucked him. You know what? I will do your family a favor and write that you were the man in bed." And he was laughing at his "joke." During all that time, I was crying hysterically, begging him to let me go, but he yelled at me and kicked me out of the office to wait outside. There was a rotten sofa in front of the office door. I was forced to wait there. Other officers were passing by, seeing me crying and wet, so they asked him, "What is going on? Why is this kid crying outside?" His answer was always, "Let him cry till he dies. He is having sex with men." One of the officers answered him, "So what? Sex is great. Let him do whatever he wants!"

When he finished writing everything he wanted to write, he took me downstairs. Eventually, we arrived at the floor of the cells. When he left, they asked me to take all my clothes off so they could check if I had anything sharp or illegal inside the cells. Taking my clothes off in front of more than eight people was terrifying. I was terrified that I could not say "No" nor refuse anything they ordered me to do. When they searched my clothes, they took my key holder and a small bottle of perfume that I always had in my pocket, and of course, my ID was sent from the gate of the building to that floor because I was officially arrested. All my stuff was put in a nylon bag with my full name on it. The full name in Syria includes the first name, then the father's name, then the family's name. I remember how much it killed me to see my dad's name in this place. Looking around me and at my full name again, I felt a pain of magma going through my veins instead of my blood. I was looking around me and thinking of "What the fuck have I brought to myself and to the people that truly love me. Instead, I brought them only shame. I will never recover from this. I do not deserve my mom or my dad. I do not deserve to be even alive."

I was taken to a cell a few minutes later. The cell was a small room with eight people inside. Everyone had his own blankets, a layered blanket to sleep on, and another to cover themselves. A tiny corner served as a toilet, with a long curtain covering it. Above that toilet was a long, narrow window to the backyard of the building. There was no space for me in the whole room except next to the toilet under the window. This window was the backyard sink. It was pouring rain outside, and a stream of sewage flowed in. One of the men gave me a black trash nylon bag to cover myself from all that water and use it as a cover for my blanket, too.

I remember covering my whole body under that blanket, which smelled like mold. I was crying in silence the entire time till I put myself to sleep. I cried silently because I couldn't let anyone sense or smell my fear. I remember every time I used to hear the lock of the cell's door opening, my heart was beating so damn fast. You connect all your dreams, wishes, and freedom to seven metallic clicks of the key in that lock.

I lost count of the time inside there, but I can tell you that I spent many hours without even a sip of water— no food, no water, not even using the toilet. Sometimes, they handed out food. The other inmates always woke me up, offering bites and water. I used to decline politely, saying, "Thanks a lot, but I am not hungry. I don't feel like eating anything." They answered, "Come on, relax, eat something, and drink some water. The first day is always hard. You will get used to it." I thought: The first day! How long am I going to stay here? What's next? No one is telling me anything. My life is over, and I am only eighteen.

I was so worried about my dad and my mom. I felt like my whole world was collapsing. My brain was trying to protect itself from exploding by thinking about what happened and what might come next. So, I started to listen to the other men's conversations. I remember hearing them whispering about how to make their confessions identical. The police were investigating corruption cases and theft of public funds. And I was asking myself a million times: Why the fuck am I here?

After losing the sense of time and giving up on the sound of the door opening for me, it did open, and the guard said my family name. I felt nothing. I was following whatever they asked me to do, but deep inside, I was preparing myself for the worst that might happen next.

They took me out of the cell, and I walked behind the guard in the hallway. I remember a creepy voice coming from one of the solitary confinements. I looked back to see a man's face with a long beard almost connected to his eyes because of how much hair he had on his cheeks. He started talking to me. "Come here. Talk to me. Why are you here?" The guard looked back and said, "Don't talk to him. He is a Salafi. We both know they hate gay people the most; if I were you, I would not even let him know what my face looks like, so keep walking."

The guard took me to the office to get my signature on several papers. When they said I must sign here and there, I was frozen - guess why? I never had a signature because I never had to sign something. The officer there said, "What's wrong with you? Hurry up. We don't have the whole day here." I told him, "Sorry, but I never signed anything before. I don't have a signature. What should I do?" He looked at me in a mean way and said, "Well, make one up right away, and you can't change it ever again. Every time you put your signature somewhere, you will relive these moments." Sadly, he was so damn right. Every time I sign something, I feel horrible, sad, and trapped again. I had to do some kid scribbling as a signature, which I never changed and will never be able to change.

They handed my belongings over to the other two officers because they were transferring me to another prison. They gave them only my key holder and said, "By the way, we took the perfume; we liked it."

I was handcuffed from behind and taken outside the building to a police station car. The two officers chatted while I was waiting in the back seat. The handcuffs were so painful because I had to sit on my palms. I tried to switch my arms to the front to ease my position, and my skinny, flexible body helped. I was able to let my legs go through my handcuffed arms quickly. When the two officers entered the car, they noticed immediately that my arms were not behind my back anymore. They started arguing about who handcuffed me in this stupid way. The one who was driving said, "You are fucking kidding me. He can choke me easily like this while driving. Are you out of your mind?" The other one answered him, "Look at him. Will this one choke you? You're fucking kidding me. If you remove his handcuffs, open the door for him, and beg him to run away, he won't, so relax, for God's sake."

They transferred me to another police station, which was in my neighborhood, and took me inside the building and downstairs right away. I was waiting there and standing for almost an hour. During this time, my dad reached out to some contacts through the family. They knew the officer in charge of the previous police station where I was officially arrested. He managed to go to his office and meet him around midnight.

That high officer was worried that it might get bigger than him because he knew what one of his subordinates had done to me. He told my dad that I was in a room, not a cell, not with prisoners but by myself, and that the room had a bed and a window. He also acted in front of my dad by calling the floor of the cells and ordering them, saying, "No one touches him or bothers him. I will break the arms of whoever does anything bad to him. Give him four if he has one blanket and send someone outside to get good food for him immediately."

My dad felt something was wrong, so he asked to see me. The officer declined "I am sorry, but it is not allowed this late. It is out of my hands. These are the rules." Of course, he declined my dad's request because I was not there anymore, and they did not even dare to tell my dad.

Years after this incident, I learned that my dad suffered a stroke and saw a doctor that day after he waited for me in the rain for hours, but still, he insisted on not letting me down and kept trying to do something for me.

At the second police station where I was transferred, I

had to be questioned again. They took me upstairs to the vice officer of the whole place. It was his night shift. When I entered his office, I noticed I could see our apartment from his windows. I could see only one corner of it: my childhood bedroom, where I dreamed of everything but this, where I realized that I was simply different from everybody else, and where I worked on accepting that fact day and night. I looked through that window, wishing nothing but to be a child again.

The officer was reading the police report of the sick homophobic officer. Then he looked at me and said, "Why are you that yellow and pale, my son!" "Because I ate nothing since yesterday morning, nor drank anything. I did not use the bathroom either. This other officer hit me and faked the report. My dad was waiting for me outside, and till now, my parents have no idea where I am." The officer said, "What? Who? Calm down, come drink some water, and tell me everything."

I told him everything. He was trying to calm me down as much as he could. He heard everything I said and commented, "They do this shit sometimes. They do this shit from time to time." He asked me where I lived. I pointed my finger at our building through the window. He called someone and said, "Here's some money. Bring him a full *Mss,hab* (grilled chicken). This is so cruel. He can barely stand on his feet. He is a child, for God's sake." Then he looked at me and said, "Son, I cannot do anything for you at this point because the report was already written over there, and it is signed by all the people who are in charge, and even your signature is beneath all the alleged confession. I will send you to court first thing in the morning, and you can tell them everything you told me. I am sure they will see what I see in you."

They took me downstairs to a room with an iron door that had a small window you could open and close from both outside and inside. The room also had a small window to nowhere and a bathroom that smelled like rotten eggs. They gave me two blankets, one to sleep on and another as a cover.

An hour later, someone opened the loud iron door to give me a bag with half of a grilled chicken wrapped in tinfoil. I said thanks, but I didn't eat anything of it. That room somehow gave me comfort, the comfort of being alone and being next to home. I was sitting there on the floor thinking of everything: my life, my family's life, my university, my friends, and myself. I started promising myself that I would never be gay again, nor straight. I just wanted to live in peace.

They brought a 14-year-old kid to the room. He was short with dark brown skin. He was Palestinian, and his parents did not give a fuck about him. We started talking, and I couldn't stop myself from asking about the reason that brought him there. He asked me first if I wanted to eat the chicken, and I told him that I was fine and the chicken was all his. While eating he told me they had caught him stealing windows from some apartment. He and his friends watched apartments on the ground floors when the owners weren't home.

They would come after midnight, remove the windows, and move them to some abandoned house in their neighborhood until they found a way to sell them on the black market. I had to ask him why he was ruining his life and not in school anymore. Was he aware of what he was doing? He responded, "I suck at school—plus, I grew up where all the people around me make their living like this, and it pays pretty well. My dad is doing his time now in prison for selling drugs. It is annoying that they will take me to the youth detention center, so I won't be with my dad."

Later, they took him out of the room somewhere upstairs. I lay awake all night in the freezing cold. I remember the pain in my teeth because of that cold; I remember the feeling of my pulse inside every one of my teeth with stabbing nerve pain. This pain was my only buddy till sunrise.

I started listening to every move around the floor in the morning because I wanted them to take me to court. It may be the end of that nightmare. I opened the small iron door window, watching every shadow passing the hallway. At some point, I could see one of the guards. So, I asked him twice with a shivering voice, "Excuse me, sir, can I know when you will take me to court?" He answered me, "Be quiet, kid. We'll take you there when we want to take you."

At that moment, someone in the cell opposite me came to the door's window. It was a woman with layers of cheap make-up and messy hair, but still, she was beautiful. She had chewing gum in her mouth. She was making a hell of smacking with that chewing gum. I could hear the echo of it all over the hallway. She scanned me with a nasty look and said, "What the fuck are you doing here? This is the room for people like me when it is their first time. What have you done? What the fuck, are you also in this business." And she laughed so loud as if she had just said the funniest joke ever. I looked at her like a pissed kid and shut the window of my door.

They took me to another room, made me hold a number, for the mugshot. I always think about this mugshot and wonder how I looked in that bad state of mind and what my eyes were saying. They took my fingerprints after the whole procedure of signing papers. One officer approached me, took me aside, and asked, "Does anyone know you are here? Do you want to call someone? Here is my phone. Call if you know one of your parent's cell phone numbers."

Sadly, I couldn't remember any of my parents' numbers. I tried to focus but was mentally exhausted, so I told him this was my dad's cell phone number, but I was not sure it was correct. After that, they took a few people, including me, to another room to prepare us for court. They were putting handcuffs on everyone. When my turn came, they realized no handcuffs were left for me. Eventually, they let it go, saying, "Look at him. This one will run away. Huh, huh, of course, he won't run away. Look at him!"

Did I think of running away? Of course, I did. Did I think about it for real? No, I did not. I knew I was already running away from something more significant than any real prison. I knew that everyone was running away from something— from different things. We always escape something—maybe a place, a place that is called home, a thought, people, or even from ourselves. I knew I was good with running away, but not from this one—I had to survive until the end, no matter what. I felt like I owed it to myself to survive. Somehow, I trusted that I was not born to be a quitter but was always born to be a winner.

During this time, my mom and dad had a feeling that I was in that specific police station, so they waited outside of the building since six in the morning. The officers crammed all the prisoners inside a white station car, including me. Everyone was normally sitting in that car except me. I had to squat back in the trunk with a glass window. I was so scared and worried that someone might see me being arrested in this humiliating way, so I hid my head between my knees the whole road to court.

My parents saw the car when it passed them next to the exit. My head was between my legs, but my parents were on the sidewalk, so they saw my head and recognized my shirt. You can imagine how painful this feeling might be for any parent and how scary the idea of your baby being taken away from you for no reason—except what the harsh laws say, and you can do nothing about it.

My mom started shouting and crying in the street. "I saw him, I saw him, just saw my baby. Why is he in the trunk? Was he moving? What have they done to my baby boy? He cannot survive this. He will always be broken from this." My dad calmed her down. "What could they do to him? He is just scared. Calm down!"

My parents stopped a cab immediately to follow the police car to know where they were taking me next. When my dad opened the cab door to jump in, his cell phone started ringing. The number I gave the officer before was correct. The officer told my dad that I was on my way to court, and he was willing to help there but wanted some money in return. Of course, my dad agreed. They decided to meet in front of the court building. They met there, and he took some money from them and asked them to wait for his call.

When I arrived at the court, they paraded us through the main building in front of everyone. Everyone was checking the group of criminals going to court that day. Everyone was checking on me as I looked much younger than the others. For me, it was a walk of shame. I was so scared that someone who knew me or knew my family would recognize me. I tried my best to be invisible as much as I could. I was staring at the floor nonstop, scared to look anyone in the eyes.

They gathered us on the floor under the building, where everyone had to wait until the judges were ready. There were two big rooms. One was for the men, and the other was for the women. They made us stand beside each other and asked our names and other questions. They started with the man next to me. "You're always in our hospitality—you won't give up the damn pimping and using women." Then my turn came, so he asked me about my name, and I answered him, feeling so ashamed that my full name was being said in a place like this. When I answered him, he said, "Ahaa, so you are the damn *Loti*." (*Loti* means a "fagot" in Arabic but is harsher than a fagot as a meaning. It came from Lot in the Old Testament, the same as Lot in the Quran, who is the prophet in Islam allegedly sent to the land of homosexuals and rapists).

When he said that, I looked to the floor and started crying like a child, replying to him only in silence. He had a black police baton in his hand. He put it under my chin and pulled my head up with the tip of it, and said, "Stop crying like a pussy. By the way, do you have a pussy? Or do you have a dick we should cut and feed to stray dogs. Just asking to know in which part of the prison you must be."

The sound of everyone laughing about the pussy joke in that vast space was so loud. I felt nothing, but my whole body and soul were shrinking; I wished I could disappear from this world. After he finished his show and made everyone's day by breaking me more, they sent us to a big room where we had to wait for the judges.

They were taking everyone upstairs one after another—except me. I stood there for almost ten hours; I remember peeling off the old, brittle, beige paint on the walls with my nails for hours and following the lines with my fingers. I was reading the small writings on the walls; some were songs, and some were just trash words, and almost everything on these walls was spelled wrong. I felt so alone and hopeless. I felt trapped there for eternity and couldn't do anything about it. So many people survive difficulties by blaming others for where they are in life or what they are going through—I did precisely the opposite. I was blaming myself for everything my parents and I were going through. I felt that *I* was the problem, because I was born gay and how I lived as a person. I just wished I could make everything terrible vanish, even if I would disappear with it all, but this is not how things work in life. Closing my eyes and ears in that place was no help because I always realized that I was there and sadly going nowhere.

Seven.

Judges usually work till three thirty in the afternoon. Around two, a guard came to the room door and said, "Hey you, hey kid, the judge in charge of your case left early. He had a work lunch." I asked, "What is that supposed to mean? What's going to happen to me now?" He said, "You will sleep in the central prison till tomorrow."

After an hour, the guard returned, opened the door, put the handcuffs on me, and said, "Come with me without saying a word." We were walking in the ample space between the rooms, and he looked around him everywhere, checking if someone was watching him. I was worried and scared, but when he took me to the bathroom, I was terrified. I feared being beaten up or even worse, being raped.

He took my handcuffs off and said, "If you talk about this to anyone, I will make your time here a living hell, you hear me? Follow me, and don't dare to go close to the door, talk with them from far, so no one will see you, and don't raise your damn voice." I followed him, feeling confused and relieved at the same time. Suddenly, I saw two people waiting on the other side of a window of the room's door. I couldn't recognize them at first. It was my mom and my dad. My vision was blurry from my tears, so I dried my eyes with both hands to see better. My mom's face was wet with tears, and my dad's look was full of worry. Seeing them in this shape ripped my heart out of my chest. The first thing they said to me was that I should be strong because I was born to be, and then they asked me if I was hungry because I looked like there was no blood in my veins anymore.

I tried my best to act strong and unbreakable, and I had everything under control. I did it so damn well, but certain people will always see beyond your skin and eyes. My mom wanted to touch me, but the guard said it was prohibited. He took me away from the door while I could hear them behind me shouting, "It is going to be over soon! don't worry, Habibi!" At that moment, my tears flowed like waterfalls—I had to turn away to avoid making my parents notice it.

It turned out they had paid money to this guard to let them see me and talk with me for less than a minute. It was a minute full of pain, relief, tears, happiness, love and worry.

I was put back in the same room I was in before. While waiting to be transferred to the central prison, two men returned to the room and started to share their stories and ask me questions. I was about to explode. I needed someone to talk to after all this time. I needed to complain to someone and open up somehow. I told them what had happened to me before, which was a huge mistake. It was one of the things in life that taught me never to trust again or open up about my problems no matter what.

During the conversation and while telling them how I ended up there, the guard showed up again and opened the door. He called my name and handed me a white bag that smelled like food from heaven. My parents had sent me two kilos of meat pies and ten Shawarma sandwiches. I found only two sandwiches in that bag; the guards had taken the rest. I had no strength to chew a bite from those sandwiches, so I gave them to the two men I talked to. They seemed open, and understanding toward what they were hearing.

Thirty minutes later, we were transferred to the central prison across the street from the court. It was a huge building with four floors and high walls surrounding it. It had this massive iron-black gate. When we entered, the guards started to perform their shakedown on us one by one inside a small room. The guard who was searching me was at the end of his twenties. He asked me about the charges that brought me there while I was taking my clothes off to be searched. I was so scared to tell, but I had to. I answered him with the word *Loata* (being a faggot), which is the common way to say it appropriately, and there was no chance to sugarcoat it.

He looked around without making eye contact or caring about it, a reaction I feared. He said, "For fuck's sake, this is why they brought you here? Who is this person who has problems with sex that bad? Sex is love, and love is sex."

We were taken out of the entrance toward the main ward in the prison, where the big dorms were located. I had to walk through the yard where all the prisoners spent their time during the day. It was obvious to everyone there that I looked so young. I tried my best not to make any eye contact. I could hear the whispering of every group we were passing by. There was a scary man with scars on his face standing with his group of inmates, who looked like the troublemakers of the whole place. The frightening man laughed and asked one of the guards taking us to the cell, "These are the newbies, no? Can we borrow the young one in our dorm only for the night? I will make it worth it; I promise!" The guard said, "Go fuck yourself, you pervert." My heart was beating so fast, and my hands were shaking nonstop. Then, we were taken to a vast room where no one was allowed to enter or leave, which made me feel a bit safer.

It was where they put the people who had not been convicted yet—the people still on trial and waiting for their sentences or those like me who had not stood in front of a judge yet. The room had huge windows, a ceiling fan, and blankets all over the floor, where around 30 men played cards or chatted. To the right was a kitchen with cooking pans and a sink with two old water taps.

At the end of the kitchen was a bathroom. An old man oversaw that place. He was reading a book and talking with no one, but you could tell he was in charge. The second I entered, the old man handed me a blanket and told me to sleep in any free space. I chose the edge of the whole room to be far from everyone. I lay on the floor and covered myself with the blanket from head to toe.

I fell asleep for a few hours. Then, the shouting and cursing of a crazy man woke me up. He cursed at everyone—the guards, the people in the room, his family, God, and the government. I was so scared of him that I didn't even dare to take the cover off my face to see what he looked like. He calmed down after a bit and started to chat with a group of prisoners. Two men in this group were the same I had told my story to. I heard someone saying, "Check on this kid. Is he alive? He hasn't moved since he came into the room. Why is he here anyway? Has anyone talked to him? He looks so young." Then one of the men I had met earlier said while laughing, "He is *Loti*, a faggot. This is his third prison in the last couple of days."

I didn't know what to do or how to move or behave. I started calming myself down and saying to myself, "What's the worst that can happen? I'm going to be fine. Everything is going to be fine. I am not here anyway. Nothing can hurt me when I am not here anymore." I cried myself to sleep.

I woke up to the same shouting and cursing from the same crazy man. He freaked out because he didn't have a blanket to cover himself with. The other men started to calm him down, and he lost it even more. He ran to where I was sleeping and pulled the blanket from above me. I was shocked but said or did nothing. I didn't even make eye contact with him. I knew he could beat me there and that I couldn't defend myself.

The old man in charge of everything there said, "What about him? He will be cold sleeping with no cover on." So, the crazy man said, "I don't give a shit, but you know what, we can share it." Which was his plan from the start. I was so scared, and I could feel something terrible was about to happen. He put the big blanket above both of us. I couldn't fall asleep for a second, but at the same time, I didn't dare to open my eyes.

He touched me with his hands under the blanket, ensuring no one in the cell was awake. He was touching my waist and my thighs. My face was turned away from his. He moved his hands slowly, trying not to wake me up. I tried my best to be in control of my whole body. If he felt something, he might think I liked it. Of course, it came to my head to say or do something, but I was scared to be in more trouble. I was the one there because of being gay, not him; I was the one that all men there felt was broken and weak, not him.

He was doing all this touching for around fifteen minutes, which felt like an eternity, and then he started trying to put his fingers under my pants from the back, which was not working. He tried to unbutton my pants in the front, and he was able to do it eventually. At that moment, I was choking with tears blocking my throat, so I coughed a couple of times. I started to cry louder. Instead of backing off, he pushed his hard dick on my bottom. I made sure that he was hearing me crying and showing him that I was having a breakdown because of what he was doing. That didn't stop him, not even a bit—it was like someone crying and scared between his arms was simply a turn-on, a hell of a turn-on. The more I cried, the more he became aggressive and horny. He harshly put his right arm around my right side and pressed his hand on my mouth to make me quieter. Then he tried with his left arm to pull my pants down. Lucky me, it was not working for him, and he was like a horny animal who had no patience to keep trying—he pulled his pants down, spat on his hand, and started masturbating on my pants from the back.

Even though I speak four languages, I am lost for words trying to find even one damn word to describe how I was feeling or how I still feel about those difficult moments of my life. I am lost for words to describe his voice while masturbating. I am at a loss for words to describe the smell of his breath under the blanket. I am at a loss for words to describe the taste of my salty tears. I am lost for words to describe the nerve-wracking sound of his cum being sprayed on my pants.

When he finished, he let go of me and started wiping his dick on my pants. I was still crying and shaking like a washed puppy—which he didn't give a shit about. He turned to the other side, pulling the blanket from above me. For him, the cover was nothing but a rape space, but for me, it was a dark and filthy space full of pain, tears, and fears.

I have been in that space before as a child. When we are adults, we process things differently from when we are children. It might affect us less badly when we have no names for things. When I was a kid playing behind our building in a park around noon, a man came close asking me for some help with his bike till he took me to a place where no one could hear us or see. As an adult, I can tell he had a fetish for seeing blood on a boy's body with tears on his face. He was dragging me around that abandoned part of the park with one hand and slapping me with the other till my cheeks, knees, and elbows were bleeding. Then he pushed me onto the floor, put his foot on my hand, and masturbated, standing above me. I went home that day and told my parents, "A man was beating me a lot, and when he stopped, he started peeing white urine." My dad was furious and swearing that he would kill this man if he knew who he was—no matter what.

I was taken to the zoo that day and spoiled for the whole summer. This is how I remembered that day as a child for so many years. I could sense the security around my parents and feel nothing but safety. In that cell, it was a different process—my parents were not around to run to, and there was no zoo to go to. I was at a human zoo with people who did not even have an iota of humanity.

When he fell asleep and snoring filled the cell, I immediately ran to the filthy bathroom, where I broke down in silence. I remember cleaning my pants on the old brown walls and slapping myself so damn hard. A part of the slapping was about how stupid I was to bring myself to all those places just to be who I am. The other part was a wake-up slapping and no time for feeling miserable and weak slapping. I remember ordering myself to be firm and pull myself together now. There was no time for pity in myself, but it's time to put faith in who I truly am and what I can survive—healing must come later.

I spent that whole night sitting in the corner of the kitchen on the floor. I was half asleep. I couldn't feel anything but unsafe in that place, but of course, I couldn't get out of it anyway. I remember hearing the birds outside, I stood up, went to the sink, washed my face with the cold water, and started walking around, waiting till the time came to take me to the judge. I counted the tiles on the floor while walking from one wall to another. I remember having nothing going inside of my head except blankness.

I was disconnected from reality somehow. When I think about it now, I can tell it was time for my brain to build an armor to feel, think, and react less to everything around me. I counted those tiles for more than five hours till the guards came to bring me out of the cell. I was taken out of the central prison with the same procedures, including the mandatory strip search. They took me to the same room on the underground floor beneath the courthouse—I had to wait again, following the lines of the cracked paint on the old walls, trying to escape reality.

At some point, a guard took me to the judge's office. My parents were waiting in the hallway. I remember my mom's eyes, devastated at seeing me in that shape and that situation. My dad was in control, always trying to make the best of the situation. When I passed them, my dad smiled and said, "Come on, Habibi, it will be fine. Things always will be fine at some point. Just be yourself, baby boy." My mom's eyes said so much, and it was enough for me.

When I entered the judge's office, I had no expectations. I saw this decent man sitting behind his desk. He had the type of face that makes you feel welcomed and safe. The second I was inside, he smiled and said, "Come in, son. Tell me everything you want to say. I got your report from the first police station and the second one, but the latter had some notes. So, tell me everything, and don't hesitate to tell me any small detail."

At that point, I started talking and talking nonstop. I told him I was beaten in the first station and how that guy wrote everything in the report as he wished. He looked at me with a face full of anger and discomfort—his eyes were watery. When I finished talking and telling him about the nightmares and daymares I had lived the last few days and keeping the rape thing to myself, one of his colleagues knocked on the office door and entered. The judge welcomed her, shook her hand, and said, "If you heard this story, your hair would stand on end. Unbelievable, unbelievable"

He asked me what I was studying, and I told him I was simultaneously studying tourism and languages at the university. He looked at me like a father and said, "The university exams are literally in four days. What are you doing here, son? Unbelievable, unbelievable." Then he asked me to go and wait outside, and when I was leaving the office, he said to me, "Good luck with your exams, son."

In the hallway. I saw one of the guards taking money from my mom because she wanted to sit next to me and hold my hands. We sat there for a few minutes, saying nothing, till one of the guards came to me and led me downstairs again.

While they were taking my handcuffs off, they asked my parents for money to "celebrate" my release—the mind games of it all. Of course, my parents gave in because they couldn't exchange their happiness for anything on earth for having me back.

We walked upstairs and then through the big building

for around five minutes. During those five minutes, I was always hiding my hands involuntarily, thinking I still wore the painful handcuffs, full of shame. I remember how much I appreciated the sun on my face the second it caressed it. The fresh air of freedom outside that building had a completely different smell. I enjoyed seeing the buildings and streets on the way home. I enjoyed walking up the stairs to our apartment. I have a gorgeous older sister I have never been close to because of our eight-year difference. When I entered home for the first time again, she ran to the door, hugged me, lifted me, and started swinging me nonstop. It was overwhelming to feel loved and safe again. I remember my first glass of water and how refreshing it was, the first meal – *Mlokheh* - my mom made me that day, and how delicious it was. I remember chatting with my whole family that evening and telling them stories from inside the prisons and how funny I could make them sound. I made everything sound much better than reality. I started to tell those stories and be the first to believe them. If we cannot change what happened, we better change how we talk about it. It helps to some point—to heal a wound, you need to stop touching it. I had to prepare for my exams because I was running out of time and did excellent in almost everything in them.

Eight.

The good and bad met simultaneously because I knew that yesterday was heavy and I had to put it down, but I always knew I had to lift it at some point. Everything changed tremendously. I had no relatives or friends anymore. Everyone I called a friend cut contact with me. Some feared being around me because they were convinced I was still being watched by the police for being gay. Some were embarrassed to talk with me even though some were gay, and they could walk in my shoes anytime. I was bullied by them for months after that. I was still on some gay chat groups of those people, and I remember sneaking online to check what they were talking about me every night. They said I had been dragged out of the house or busted for having orgies on the beach at night and that I was beaten before being arrested. They also said they broke my teeth and burned me with cigarettes, so now I would look ugly, and my face would be deformed.

For many nights, I was reading all this trash about myself and feeling sad because I thought we could be a hell of an army for each other. But again, gay people in those societies are the first enemies of each other.

One of those people was a distant relative of mine and a neighbor of my parents in the village. He was going around the gay scene telling everyone that I had been dragged from home and that my mom had tried to stop them, so they had pushed her on the floor while they were laughing at the "fag" son, referring to me.

I went through a heavy depression during those six months. I had so many breakdowns that I lost count, the type of breakdowns that made me almost pass out and let my mouth foam. Did I think of killing myself or harming myself? Hell no. I knew I had to be my own army. I knew that it was my story, not anyone else's. I knew I was the artist of my own life, and I wouldn't hand the paintbrush to anyone else— especially those poisonous people. A while later, I started working out at home every day because I realized that I had to take care of my body; at the end of the day, it was the only place I had to live in. In a few months, my body shape changed significantly; my shoulder got wider, and my chest fuller. I didn't look like a child anymore—especially with my beard.

During summer, I started to be in touch with my old friends, who were also my neighbors. They used to come to my place, or I went to theirs. There were only a few floors between us, so I was always under my parents' eyes. Once, we decided to go to a coffee place after university, and it was the first time I hung out with friends in a long time.

When we were there, my close friend noticed one of the gay friends I had before on the other table with a bunch of girls. I couldn't recognize him at first because of the plastic surgeries he had done to his face. His sister was there too, and when she noticed us, she came saying hi. Then her brother came too. We ended up sharing the same table and chatting all together.

Mo was the gay friend who always called me his "Best friend and brother." He used to sleep over at my place, wear my clothes, and make pizza with my mom—and who also disappeared when I needed a friend. He tried to fix things between us that day, but I couldn't accept him immediately. At least we decided to stay in touch.

During the next five weeks, he called me a dozen times, but I ignored his calls because I had no trust in gay people in general. One evening, I was listening to "Fighter" by Christina Aguilera, and suddenly, I felt so fed up with the whole world, including myself. I started to be pissed at myself because of how much time I had lost in the last half of the year—feeling self-pity and struggling with nightmares and flashbacks, while the true me would never let anything or anyone design my own life for me—when to be scared and of what, or to live in fear and sorrows all the time. Thinking about that, I said, "It is okay that I forgot who I am for a while. Anyway, Welcome back."

Mo called me, and I answered him. He told me he was going to the beach with a few friends to smoke Shisha and asked me to join them. I hesitated a lot before deciding that I had to go. I was telling myself, "What am I scared of? People talk. They will trash me or talk behind my back no matter what." I showered, got ready, and took a cab to the beach.

When I arrived, I could see more than twenty guys sitting at a big table, throwing jokes at each other and laughing as always. I stood far away from them, asking myself, "Am I sure I want to return to this? Or am I sure I want to return to this scene?"

I pulled myself together, "What's the worst that could happen? I still have my sharpened tongue to defend myself with, and If I feel uncomfortable—I can always leave."

I kept walking toward the table slowly and confidently, like in old times. When they noticed me, everyone started whispering in each other's ears. I said to myself, "Here we go. It is like I left them an hour ago. They will never change."

When I arrived, everyone went quiet. I sat next to Mo, and on his other side were twins he had met online. He was planning to have an orgy with them later. I already knew some of the people there, so they left their seats and came to hug me, gave me the three traditional kisses, and told me how much I had changed and that I looked so handsome.

Mo raised his voice so everyone could hear him on the table and said, "For everyone who doesn't know him, he is my best friend and a family to me." It was a catchy speech for me for only a second because I immediately remembered that no one comes before dicks in his life. At the same time, I remembered that I had accepted this about him years ago.

 I was quiet most of the time, and at some point, they decided to play their favorite game: "Honesty." They placed a bottle on the table and twirled it around. The rules are simple: When the head of the bottle stops in the direction of a person, this person should ask a question that everyone should answer. Usually, they are serious questions. Before starting the game, the group came up with some other rules. Whoever didn't answer the questions must leave the table immediately. Some of them were worried about that as they knew the questions would be mean and heavy, and the last thing they wanted was to look weak or nervous because they would be under *shacher*.

Shacher means reading someone in the gay scene in a mean, funny, or sarcastic way. Usually, it is speaking badly and meanly. The accurate word in English to describe it should be "bullying." Whoever is mastering this in the gay scene will be respected more, but only in his face, not behind his back.

When they started playing the game, the bottle's head stopped in the direction of an older guy whom I never met before. He looked at everyone and said, "I will go easy on you kids. Let's start with something smooth to turn the jealousy on around this table. I can smell the gasoline, so I'll turn on the matches." Everyone laughed about what he said, including me, because jealousy is simply a reality between gays—at least in that scene.

He asked a question that sounded at least not mean or heavy. The question was: "Who do you find the hottest on this table? And you better not say your own names, ladies." Everyone got excited to answer, but you could see how uncomfortable they were because they already felt bad. What if no one said their names? I answered first and said "Mo" because he was the closest, and I didn't want to be a part of their "One hit on the other"-game. They started answering in a circle that ended with Mo. More than seventeen responded with my name, including the twins, and the rest chose Mo.

When they said my name, most glanced at Mo and explained why. "Come on, he changed a lot," they said. For me, it was nothing but typical gay mind games. For Mo, it pissed him off because of the twins he wanted to have sex with. He barked at them, "So you met me online, and now you're hitting on my friend. You better vanish from my life after we leave this table." The twins laughed because they thought it was some joke, so he said, "What's so fucking funny here? I am not fooling around with you two. Do you think that he's interested in you now? He does not give a shit about guys like you."

I stayed quiet as I knew how things always ended up with Mo. He will always find a way to play with situations to be in control. It became tense, and everyone went silent except the older guy who had asked the question. He was staring at his cell phone and laughing. At some point, he stood up and said, "My job is over here. Hopefully, I made some of you laugh. We meet to learn more shit about each other. We feed on it."

Which I agree with. Most of their lives are all about dressing up, bragging about it, having sex with as many men as they can, trashing each other, and harming other people's lives. I witnessed a few times how some of them would put some drugs inside the person's bag they hate the most and call the police, or they would go to someone's workplace, make a scene for him there, screaming around that he is gay. Most of those incidents ended badly—usually, they went to the person's workplace wearing makeup and dressing like women so it would be easier to get the person in trouble. They brag about this behavior, calling it *"Aadarah,"* which means somehow "mightiness." For some, it is a way of showing that they can run this shit show.

At that table, things turned awkward, so everyone was finding an excuse to leave—me included. I told Mo I couldn't stay out late tonight and had to go. He came close to my ear and said, "Don't be a party pooper. I have not seen you for almost a year, so let's go to the internet café." It was popular for gays to go to this kind of place. It was before the times of Wi-Fi and data on smartphones. I told him, "No, really, what party exactly am I missing? I better go home. I don't want to stay late." So, he said, "Whatever, I am coming to your place then." In Syria, it is not polite to simply turn someone away. So, I told him, "Let's meet another time; I have to wake up early." He said, "Come on, I won't stay long." This was typical Mo. He was so insistent and such a control freak. At last, he just invited himself over.

We sat on the balcony, chatting and remembering old times. Suddenly, he said, "So tell me, did the police ask you about me when you were arrested." I said to myself, "You're fucking kidding me; even with this— it is all about you. This is the first thing you ask me instead of: How are you doing now? Or: Are you okay after all of this?" But instead, I answered him, "Yeah, they did ask me about you. They wanted to take your autograph." "I bet they did. Were there any hot men inside?" I said, "The last thing you want on earth is to go through what I have been through." He said, "Come on, you are dramatic." He continued, "Everyone was talking shitty stories about you in the gay scene, and I defended you all the time."

The truth is that Mo was the one who spread the story of me having broken teeth and a deformed face. I said, "Ah, really? Thanks!" He left shortly after, and we lost touch for a few weeks, but right the next day, he removed me from all the gay chat groups where they talked shit about me.

During the next few months, I started to befriend everyone in the gay scene again. I was stupid enough to trust them once more and act like I would never be embarrassed of my community, no matter what. It was out of rebellion and anger at the same time. I received a letter that I should attend court again to be released without serving any time in prison for being gay. The first time, I couldn't hire a lawyer because of the homophobic police officer who had written the forged report claiming I had confessed, so there has not been a job for a lawyer to defend me there. This time, I was able to do that, and I did it. I was worried and terrified to go back to that place again. I couldn't talk about it or discuss it with anyone.

At the end of that summer, I had to quit my tourism studies because I couldn't afford the lawyer fees. I only saw the lawyer once, and after that, he delayed the hearings and got paid. I wanted to focus on my language studies and job, which I was doing well.

I taught international students studying Arabic literature and translated almost everything in their classes. During that time, I was earning well. I used to do some sort of therapy—by buying things and spending money on friends. I remember that if I called one of them to meet for lunch or dinner or drinks or even for Shisha and they said they couldn't go out because they were out of money, I used to tell them to take a cab, and I would pay for it and for everything they would order. I was trying too much not to make them feel that having some money changed me. The thing was that they knew this and took advantage of it. They started to do it on purpose, and the sentences "I would love to, but I am broke." or "It would be amazing, but I am out of money." became a habit.

It was a time when I had to pretend to be someone else, someone who must be flat and doesn't care about anything. A person who can do nothing but play the role of someone else, or otherwise, will be cast out and be an outsider.

During the same period, I met my first boyfriend, who was in his late twenties. He was an Emirati British who lived between many places, taking care of his family's companies. We met once at a restaurant where he was rude to me, and then he paid someone to get my number.

Let me tell you a little bit about him. Saif was raised in a family where he was taught never to take No as an answer for what he wants. He always knew what he wanted and worked on getting it no matter how much power or money it would cost. He always surrounded himself with people he knew were around only to get something from him, and he enjoyed that. For him, it was a game of controlling people and giving them some things they wanted in return. It was the game of sitting at a table with many people and acting like the center of the world.

Was I in love with him? No, I was not. Did I love things about him? Of course, I did. Did I have feelings for him? I certainly had—otherwise, I couldn't lose my virginity and be with him for around three years. Was he in love with me? He certainly was. He was surrounded by guys who were his type and wanted to achieve the life he had. He infused it into most of them in small doses, as small as drops. With me, he tried that with floods. He said, "You are the only one who said No to me without hesitation. You are the only one who did it without considering what you might lose. You are the only one who faced me with my ugly behavior. How can I not love you while you are the only one who is not easy, and I cannot control!"

Later in my life, I realized that it had started as a game to prove that no one can play hard to get with him, and I did that pretty well to Saif. He tried almost everything to be with me, and with time, I enjoyed the trying and the attention. I did it only because I was not ready to be in any relationship. I was not prepared to love someone else besides myself. I needed to love myself the most first, then others.

While playing his game, he fell in love with me, but with his own rules. He wanted nothing to change in his life at all but wanted to add something more to it. That something was me. He loved me, yes, but this is not the whole thing. Love means being faithful, and giving care and security. For me, he failed with all the above.

I always knew he might be cheating on me and ignored it. Our friends did everything to prove it to me. They did that not out of anything except hurting us, hurting me because I was being cheated on, and hurting him because he loved me.

Saif and Mo hated each other and acted like they couldn't sit at the same table. Eventually, Mo met someone online from Dubai, and they only started dating for a few weeks. His guy decided to take him there so they could be next to each other. Mo told me while preparing his move to Dubai, "Fuck him. I just want to be in Dubai, and then I can meet whoever I want and do whatever I wish." For me, Mo was a teenager who was always on fire to meet people, have sex, and do whatever he wanted, so I never took what he said seriously.

Mo needed more money to book his flight to Dubai and to buy some stuff. He called his guy and asked him for some cash. His guy said, "I paid enough so far for you. You must deal with this alone to prove you are serious about us." I remember Mo freaking out like crazy after that phone call. He started crying and complaining about his life. I offered to pay for his flight, and he would pay me back when he started working there.

I remember the day before his flight from Damascus Airport. None of his family or any of his friends wanted to go there to say goodbye to him. I felt bad for Mo. He knew I would come to Damascus with him to say goodbye. I just wanted him to leave with good memories of kindness. I invited more than twelve of our friends to come to Damascus, and I paid for the road, the hotel, and everything. At that period of my life, friendships were the things I wanted to work on and invest in the most.

Two days after Mo left to Dubai, Saif called me, and we had an argument that ended like so many times before, but with a bit of a stronger tone that time. I remember saying to him, "You know what? We are over. I will change my cell phone number; you better not try to get it. I can't take this toxic relationship anymore."

A week later, Mo in Dubai blocked me on Facebook and my number. It was tough for me to lose two important people simultaneously for no apparent reason. Saif eventually got my number and called me to get us back together, saying he was so sorry and never meant anything like this to happen. At that time, I was already in a new relationship, but I could feel that something was on the top of his tongue, so I asked him, "Is there something more you want to say?" At that moment, he started crying and said, "Never meant to do that to you. Maybe he did. Actually, for sure, he did." So, I said, "I am lost here and know you are drunk, but I have never seen or heard you crying. What's going on? And who is he you're talking about?" He said, "I am sure your friends told you." "No one told me anything. What are you talking about?" "That Mo and I were having sex even before you broke up with me. When he came to Dubai, he told me so much shit about you, and out of jealousy, I believed everything."

I was speechless for a few minutes while Saif was

crying. I hung up and turned my phone off. I felt betrayed and lost. I thought of all the nights I felt terrible for losing them together. It turned out I lost them simply for each other. I realized that the only person I ever lost and needed back was *me*, just *me* and nobody else. I realized that my biggest mistake was letting people stay around me far longer than they deserved. After a few hours, I calmed down a bit and turned on my cell phone again, and the first thing that showed up on my phone's screen was a text message from Saif begging me to let him fix things and not to cut him off. I still remember my reply: "I cut you off because you simply handed me the scissors!" I never heard from Saif again.

The next day, Mo called me, and I answered him icily, so he asked, "What's going on? Why are you in this shitty mood?" "*You* better tell me about that because Saif called me today and told me everything." He asked, "What do you mean with everything?" "He told me about you two." "Oh God, I thought you knew already. Everyone knew that. It was no secret. All your old neighborhood gay friends you meet daily knew about it. For me, it meant nothing, sweetheart. He used to be just like any escort client for me. We used to meet, fuck, and I got money from him." "This is all you have to say about it; for real?" Mo said, "It is such an old story. Stop acting like you hate me now. Don't be dramatic!" "He was my boyfriend, and now he is not. I thought you were my best friend, and guess what? You are not anymore. Believe me; I do not hate you. I wish you had no one as a friend except if they are just like you." He answered, "So you will cut all these years of friendship because of a guy!" I said, "I am not losing a friend when it comes to you—I just realized I never had one!" This day was one of many in my life when I repeatedly said that I should not cling to the world but *be* the world. I knew I should stop watering dead plants and move on. No best friend would do me good, better than me.

Nine.

It was March 25, 2011. I was nineteen years old. It was the Friday that changed everything; it was the day that changed everything for the worse. The one that brought more fear and terror to my life, the people I love, and their lives. The one that brought all the doubts in the universe, the belief that nothing will change for the better, and hope is simply a philosophical lie. It tore open so many wounds that won't seem to heal—the start of the pain that was so damn real. There was just too much that time couldn't erase.

I walked downtown with my friend Lara in the afternoon to meet another friend. The more we came closer to the square downtown, the more we saw people running in and out of that area. We were still trying to understand what was going on. Fridays and Saturdays are the days of the weekend in Syria. All stores are closed only on Fridays except during specific days like Christmas, New Year's Eve, Eid, Mother's Day, and Teacher's Day. That Friday was none of the above.

There was a bridge that we had to cross. When we reached the highest point, we could overlook the square, where a huge crowd had gathered. Law enforcement surrounded the whole square, not letting other people enter. Some parts of the surrounding buildings were on fire. It was surreal, and we could still not understand what was happening.

Our friend, whom we were supposed to meet in that square, called us. She was talking with a shaky voice. She was passing the square when a group of men left the Mosque after Friday's prayers, started protesting, and became quickly violent. They started attacking the stores and breaking in. She got scared during this and entered a building to hide inside. She was so frightened that she begged us to try to come and get her, which was impossible.

We left the bridge and walked slowly toward the law enforcement. We were shocked and terrified at the same time. A man was carrying a baby with his wife—they stopped us and said, "Where are you going? Don't you see what's going on? Go back. It is not safe there." We told him what was happening and why we were trying to get closer to the square. He said, "Oh my God, I will walk with you there without your friend here. It is unsafe for you."

Someone inside the building where we stood was listening to us from the second floor. When the man asked his wife to take their baby and go home immediately, the person listening to our conversation threw a heavy metal pipe at us. I still remember how it fell so fast, crossing the few feet of space between my face and Lara's. We looked up to check where it fell from and why it fell on us—there was no one on the windows or balconies we could see. The man, still holding his crying baby, started shouting and cursing, "What the fuck is wrong with you people? There's a toddler, for God's sake!" A woman with a scarf covering half her face put her head out of a window and shouted, "Allah Akbar, Allah Akbar. You deserve more, you whores and pimps. Allah Akbar, Allah Akbar." Lara yelled back at her, "You're the damn whore! You're the one who almost killed one of us. There's a baby!" The woman spat out of the window on us and said, "Women like you who dress like this, showing half their bodies, are whores and infidels. Allah Akbar on people like you."

This attitude might be a massive problem for some people, and that religious woman insulting us was undoubtedly one of them. No one of us said another word, and we walked away immediately. No one of us had dealt with religious people before. We thought they stayed in their small circles. We were so wrong about that. That day, they started to show themselves more in the spotlight.

The Friday after was even scarier. I remember around five in the afternoon, my friends and I were sitting in the garden, and we heard heavy shooting. Everyone in the neighborhood rushed outside to their balconies or even the streets. We joined them. A red car was speeding, and the guy sitting next to the driver held a long gun pointed outside the window. The car disappeared at the end of the street.

Rumors made the rounds in the whole neighborhood. Everyone started explaining and acting like they knew what was happening. While in reality, no one knew shit, and everyone was stunned by what happened. You could feel the tension, the fear, and the confusion on everyone's faces.

Later, a motorcycle showed up in the middle of the main street, and the driver started talking with the people, saying, "The religious people from the Sunni neighborhood are coming toward here carrying knives and wooden sticks." The majority in my neighborhood was predominantly Alawi and Christian.

The man on the motorcycle left, and we never saw him

again. Men like him were going from one area to another, telling people they would be attacked. The plan was to plant mistrust and fear between them according to their religion and sect. At the start of the problems, educated individuals oversaw things, so this plan did not work. The *Mkhtars* played a crucial role. A *Mkhtar* is a position for a man or a woman who is usually old, respected, and knows everyone who lives in a specific area.

I remember my neighborhood's *Mkhtar* talking on the phone with his counterpart from the Sunni neighborhood, the man on a motorcycle had talked about. They decided to walk on the main street until they would meet in the middle. My friend and I were on my balcony on the sixth floor, watching them from above. I remember a group of people walking behind those two old Mkhtars from both sides till they met in the middle, shook each other's hands, and said loudly, "We are all brothers and sisters, same blood, different beliefs, and that's fine." And the two big groups started marching in the street, shouting, "Syria comes first! Syria comes first!"

I grew up with the credo, "Religion and faith are only for God, and the home country is for everyone." I loved this and still do. They also say, "Your freedom ends when it might harm the freedom of others." And I loved this saying even more. For me, no one can tell anyone else what to believe or wear as long as there's no harm to a soul in any of it.

On the night of the same day, things went out of control. First, there were rumors that snipers were positioned on top of some buildings, especially abandoned ones or those under construction. People were spreading this around, and no one believed it. After all, we were not living in a damn action movie.

Sadly, it was worse. Eventually, people had to realize they were going through similar events, but in the damn reality. The word about the snipers became increasingly serious when the police started to show up in every neighborhood and announced they had already arrested a few of them. The police asked for the people's help by forming neighborhood watch groups in every part of the city.

In my neighborhood, it was decided that one person from every family should be down in the street. My parents had already retired and moved to the village at that time. I was living with my older brother. All his friends enlisted for the neighborhood watch. People had no weapons, so they held wooden sticks and improvised tools. They placed chairs on the sidewalks and drank coffee and tea. At first, everyone dealt with it as a fun thing full of adrenaline. It seemed to be some night gathering for men till a black Kia car entered the street speeding, chased by the police.

The people in my neighborhood started to realize it was not their safe Syria anymore and felt like they were in some criminal gangster simulation. People were stunned by what just happened. The sound of the bullets from far away broke people's nerves. I remember how worried and scared I was for my brother. Seeing him down the street holding nothing to protect himself and how shocked and nervous he was. I still remember how he shouted at me from down the road to the balcony on the sixth floor. "Go inside and stay away from the windows!"

The feeling of that night will always be real and scary, but at the same time, I cannot explain the fog inside of my head. It was real. And it was happening.

Around four in the morning, another car drove through the main street. Inside sat three men and a woman armed with rifles pointed out of the windows to the sky. The men from the neighborhood watch wanted to run toward the car but hesitated once they noticed the rifles. One in the car shouted, "You stay away, people! We don't want to kill any of you, so don't make us!" He didn't speak with any Syrian accent, so he must have been a stranger. The car sped out of the street, and a cautious calm invaded the whole place.

I brought a small mattress and laid it out on the

balcony. No one could sleep that night. The whole next day, the neighborhood watch stayed in the streets. My brother and his friends switched with other people to do shifts. He was not even able to open his eyes anymore, so he went to bed to get some rest. Less than twenty minutes later, someone from the night watch called my brother on his cell phone and told him they had observed a person carrying a long bag entering our building. I remember my brother tiptoeing through the living room toward the apartment door, armed with a broomstick. I asked, "What's going on?" He looked at me with tired red eyes. "They think a sniper entered our building."

Our apartment had a big, long balcony; anyone could access it through the roof. At that moment, a million thoughts crossed my mind: What if he jumped onto our balcony? What if he shoots my brother in front of me? What if I am the one who will be shot? What if he takes us hostage? What's going to happen? What should we do?

Meanwhile, the police were on the way, and some men from the neighborhood watch were coming upstairs with wooden and metal sticks. My brother opened the apartment door and started whispering to the others. Suddenly, some cracking sounds were coming from the rooftop. No one could do anything about it. Everyone did their best to calm down.

When the police arrived, they asked us to go inside our apartment and sent two officers to our balcony; two stayed in the hallway, and two went to the rooftop. When they reached the roof, they couldn't find anyone. There are always water containers on the rooftops of buildings in Syria. The police had to check around and between them. After a few minutes, we heard someone shouting. "What the fuck are you doing here? Raise your arms!"

They arrested a Syrian man with an eastern accent, common in the area next to the borders to Iraq. He had a rifle, a small gun, and anti-sleeping pills. We never knew in detail what his confessions were. Still, a foreign sniper woman got arrested inside an abandoned building nearby. Someone from the neighborhood helped capture her before the police arrived. He recorded her. In that video, she says, "You saw nothing yet, people. The coming is greater and worse. Trust me that you have seen nothing yet. Wait till you see the assassinations, suicide bombings, and the kidnapping." And this was exactly what would happen all around the country soon.

I was never a fan of politics. I always disliked it. For me, politics meant, most of the time, a bunch of people who wear fancy suits and expensive clothes. Everything they do follows a script. Whenever they do something that looks good, cameras should be somewhere around. Reaching more power and getting more voters and supporters is all that matters, as well as controlling the lives and decisions of an entire population. Religion still plays a significant role. Pressing some religious people's buttons to turn them into radicals became a trend in the last decades.

In short, I was never a follower. I never could follow someone or something other than my brain and guts. I always believed in God, but following a religion was never my thing. I respect every religion and its beliefs as long as there's no harm to others. I have never entered a mosque but have gone to many churches. I loved the architecture, the vibes of peace inside, and the idea of lighting a candle to be closer to God. I never saw God or the universe as someone or something to fear or as a punisher. I always believed that we are humans who might be cruel and unjust. The bad and good are within every one of us. So, let's not put it on someone else, someone no one can see.

Later, in the summer of 2011, many people I knew or were my close friends tried their best to be a part of the change against corruption and get better rights. But they walked away from the protests quickly. One said, "We all went there together, believing it would be peaceful and with nothing but meaningful requests behind it. We were marching. Everything seemed so moving and connecting until we noticed some people with knives and *Shintianeh* (A sharp tool made of Aluminum in the shape of a belt that troublemakers wear as a weapon for street fights). We all were there in different parts of the protest. We all saw those people with nothing but hatred and troubles inside their heads. We had to walk away immediately because this didn't represent us."

The media never talked about any of that. They did everything to help create the monsters that ate and still eat Syria from every side. During that same summer, things went back to normal downtown. There were a few coffee places where gay people met. They were known in the whole city as the coffee places of the gays. In summer or during good weather, the owners of those coffee places put some tables on the square's sidewalk. I was sitting at one of them with a couple of friends, checking the news online on my phone, and I still remember getting a notification from one of the most famous news channels in the world. The report read: "Live from the square of **** in Syria. Peaceful protesters shot and killed by the police." It was precisely where I had been sitting since the morning and where I was having coffee with my friends at that exact moment. The square around me was full of ordinary people and kids. People were going to work, some were shopping, and some were sitting in cafes around the square. Nothing at all of what they were streaming was happening.

Their live streaming lasted more than three hours. They brought a few political analysts for statements. They interviewed witnesses who were around this protest. For just a few seconds, stop thinking of all the reports you saw on media or social media about Syria and try to answer my question. Remember that only you hear your answer. What would you do if you were walking in my shoes in your country?

People were fed with the illusion that Syria was being liberated, while the reality is that Syria was drowning more and more in quicksand at the hands of Syrians themselves with the help of half of the globe.

I had an amazing friend, Ziad, whom I had known since I was nine. We shared the same desk at school for almost seven years. Even though we were always close friends, we used to lose contact occasionally. The last time I saw him, I wanted to come out to him, and I knew that nothing would change in our friendship. I trusted him and trusted the human and the good in him. I was never able to come out to him as gay ever.

The last time we met, it was all about him. He was broken and sad after he and his girlfriend broke up. His dad never liked her, nor did his girlfriend's parents like him. He ended the talk about this by accepting everything and said, "We are not meant to be together. Maybe one day we might be." He decided to join the army to be away from everyone: his family, his friends, and the love of his life. His service was next to the Syrian-Turkish border on the sides of a town called Kasab. One morning, I got a message from Ziad's sister that he was kidnapped with his friends. A man had called them asking for a lot of money as a ransom, or they would send his head for them in a box. I immediately went to their house. Everyone cried when I arrived; his mom passed out every few minutes. When she opened her eyes, her wailing began, "No, not my only son! No, not the half of my heart!"

Ziad's family tried calling the kidnappers. The number didn't respond. A couple of hours after midnight, the family finally got a message. Everyone looked at each other, terrified to check their phones. It was a video of some man asking, "What is your name, you animal?" We watched the footage of Ziad being questioned by these men. His face was covered with bruises. The kidnapper asked again, "What is your name, you animal?" Ziad was standing, looking at the ground in silence. The man shouted at him, "Curse at *Ali bin Abi Talib*!" (Ali bin Abi Talib is the cousin of Prophet Mohammad and his son-in-law. He is also a holy figure of wisdom for Alawis). Ziad was an Alawi. "And why would I do that?" "Because I said so, you infidel!"

Out of nothing, he took the gun, pointed it at Ziad's forehead, and shot him with two bullets. It took me many months to pull myself out of the floods of depression. I searched for a reason why humans can become so inhumane. At some point, I realized my reasoning would not give me any answers.

During that time, I was always curious about the international media, what they were showing, and what not about the unfolding drama in Syria. There were big demonstrations in some places across the country, aired internationally for weeks. People chanted only one sentence in Arabic. "Alawis are going only to the coffins, and the Christians will be kicked out of Syria to Beirut!"

Seeing this on international channels from countries with so much freedom and respect for all sorts of things, with the idea of being human, having the freedom of speech, and so much more, airing this without having a clue about what's been chanted in these demonstrations was indescribable. All I had inside my head was, "Shame on everyone who supports this!" Meanwhile, the official Syrian channels only aired documentaries about the penguin mating season, with thousands being tortured in prisons all around the country.

One day, I got a phone call from an unknown number. The guy talking was someone I knew from the gay scene. He told me I should watch my back. When I asked for the reason, he answered, "Your full name is right in front of me. No one wanted to tell you this first and warn you, but your name is on a blacklist of a radical Islamist group." With that blacklist, they wanted to "cleanse the society." I laughed and said, "You are kidding. Why?" They had put me on this list because I was gay and had posted my face pictures on gay dating apps.

Did I freak out? Of course, I did. Did I change anything about my lifestyle? Hell no, I did not. I was somehow proud that my face and who I was were bothering them so much that they put me on their blacklist to kill or kidnap me. I didn't take it that seriously until I started receiving many strange messages on gay dating apps. Those messages from all these different accounts sounded precisely the same and were obviously written by the same people. They were trying to meet me as soon as possible. They asked me all types of fishy questions. I started receiving phone calls from people who used to curse and bark with threats to harm me or my family. I had no choice but to change my phone number and get rid of the old one because of all those threats, which haunted me for a long time.

2014 was the year when the Syrian regime agreed to give up chemical weapons under the deal with the Organization for the Prohibition of Chemical Weapons. The plan was that all the chemical weapons would be transferred from their bases through the ports of the coastal cities. They were transported in massive trucks. During each transport of those weapons through the city of Latakia, the rebels shot the city with dozens of missiles launched from areas next to the Turkish borders in the north, putting almost a million and a half Syrians in huge danger.

On the day of one of the last transports, I was about to meet my cousin Sarah and her new boyfriend. Sarah had just turned twenty-six years old and was starting to do her PhD in English literature. She was about to leave the university when one of those missiles landed a few meters away. Sarah died on the way to the hospital. Sarah was intelligent, ambitious, gorgeous, and one of the sweetest people I ever knew. Sarah is gone.

Sarah's professors at university hung a picture of her in every class. So many people came to her funeral. Sarah is gone. Everyone accepted this somehow except her father. He began to sing on the balcony of their small house every day around the time she used to return home. In the first year, he sang so many different songs for her to come back, making everyone who heard him tear up. The year after, he started to sing only one song for her. Eventually, he had to stop singing for Sarah, or maybe Sarah just stopped singing out of him.

Ten.

I met a man on one of the gay dating platforms I was on. We felt pretty good chemistry between us from the start. The problem was that he lived on the other side of the world. He was an American, and he could travel almost everywhere he wanted. Still, being Syrian, I was banned from entering every country on earth without a visa, a visa that was requested from me for nothing but being born in a place I had never chosen.

Jack was almost forty years old when we met each other online. He lived in New York City, where he worked in real estate. Jack was a friendly, caring, determined, and smart guy. We started talking on Skype every Sunday evening and later every single day on the phone. We got used to each other. I remember waiting for his call every evening. We used to share our daily lives like this for almost two years. We were not dating anyone else during this period, even with the distance between us. Have we ever said, "I love you"? No, not really. We both knew it needed more.

Eventually, I managed to get approval to leave Syria so we could meet. It took a lot of my savings to handle the corruption. I was without a job then because I lost all my international students the second the war broke out in Syria. I managed to keep a few young students, kids from families who had escaped to my city, to whom I gave English lessons for free.

I arrived in Istanbul after flying via Beirut. I was scared and nervous about anything that might go wrong, especially since it was my first time traveling outside Syria. Jack stood in the arrival hall waiting for me with a bouquet of roses. When I saw Jack, I felt safe and protected because of who he was and because he was an American citizen who wouldn't let anything wrong happen to me. I remember feeling genuinely free for the first time as a young gay guy. I remember running to hug him. I forgot where I was. We kissed on the lips in front of so many people. I didn't care anymore.

In the cab, we just looked at each other. It felt unreal. At that moment, Jack said, "I love you." The bad thing was that I was not feeling the same. It became a bit awkward that I didn't say it back. I felt he was okay with that, which made me feel good. The second we arrived at the hotel room, I had to call my mom, who was sick then. She had lung problems and underwent surgeries on both eyes. It all happened so fast, right after my flights had been booked, so I couldn't cancel them. I could feel my mom was convinced I would never return to Syria. She cried a lot before I left, thinking she might never see me again. I remember promising her I would never do such a thing without telling her. She acted like she believed me, but she never did.

Jack knew about all of this. After talking with my mom to tell her I had arrived safely, Jack and I opened a bottle of champagne to celebrate meeting each other. Jack took his first sip of champagne and said, "So I said I love you, and you said nothing, but it is okay because you are still young. Anyway, I have a proposal for you. What about if we get married in the US embassy this week, and you wait a bit here for the visa, and then we can live together in New York." I was stunned. "What? I don't get it. Get married?" "Yes, we can get married this week. I called the embassy and asked about everything." So, I asked, "When did this happen? You never told me any of this?" "You are handsome, and I am handsome. We fit together perfectly, so you have no reason to say no. And do not take Syria, your family, and especially your mom's situation as a reason for saying no. I love you, and I mean it. You do not love me yet, but you will. I can give you more than your mom ever gave you. You have no future in Syria. Don't be a fool ruining your life by staying in a place that will destroy you." I said, "Don't you feel you are coming too fast and strong on me? And who are you exactly to compare yourself to my mom? You are talking with me like I am doomed, and you are the savior." "I know I am coming fast on you with all of this, but you have to realize that you will be nothing without me and what I can give you." I answered, "I am nothing for you. You just said you love me, so you are in love with Mr. Nothing." "No, you are not nothing; you are an amazing guy who wants to keep living in his miserable country a miserable life with a family that prevents him from living in a better place." "Don't you dare to call my country miserable and say that my family doesn't want the best for me. Right now, I feel like I am learning what I should really learn about you." His answer was, "Let's talk about it tomorrow. What about we have sex now?" "No way, this is some joke. Are you fucking serious?"

I said to myself, "Look around you. You are not in your home country. You cannot just go home. You are not even staying in a hotel room under your name." I locked myself in the bathroom. I thought about the situation I had gotten myself into and how much time I spent dreaming of a person. I thought about everything he had said. We always avoid the ugly truth, don't we?

At some point, he knocked on the door to apologize and try to fix things. I left the bathroom, and he hugged me tightly, saying, "I got used to the idea that you are in my life, and I know you are the one, but I need you to put me first somehow. I want you in my life." So, I told him, "That is sweet to say, but I am not sure if I can love you without trusting you again." The whole drama was not even mentioned the next few days, but he brought the topic up again two days before my flight back. He was trying to break my confidence first in case I decided to go back. He started to body-shame me: I was too skinny and almost looked ill. He assured me he would nevertheless find me hot. Instead of trying to gain my trust again, he rummaged through my clothes and luggage every time I showered. Once, while walking around downtown Istanbul, we saw a woman wearing a Hijab. Her face was barely visible. She was sitting on the sidewalk where she placed her Syrian passport on the floor in front of her to beg for money. When we passed her, he stopped and whispered, "Look, do you see your friend? This is exactly what you might do if you go back." I was shocked by what he said, but it made me defensive with him.

When he opened the topic of his marriage proposal again two days before my flight, we had a heated argument. This time, he raised his voice in my face, repeating everything he had said the first time. At that point, I couldn't take it anymore. I started packing my luggage while arguing with him to the point that I couldn't hear his voice anymore. I left everything there, took my wallet and passport, ran outside the room, and rushed out of the hotel.

I planned to escape to the airport and stay there for two days until my flight. I looked at the map next to the tram station and understood nothing. After fifteen minutes, Jack came to the station crying and apologizing, assuring me he never meant anything he told me. "You are too sensitive," was his verdict. The following two days passed quietly. It was clear that everything was over between us. We had lunch together on the day of my flight, and he tried to talk about it again, but I shut the topic down as quickly and peacefully as possible. When I was waiting at the airport check-in, he tried to bring it up for the last time but with an angry tone. I just kissed him again and walked away, saying, "Let's only remember what we loved about each other." All I could see in his eyes was the awareness that he had ruined everything in a few days. I walked away, never looking back, not physically or emotionally. They say you might forget what bad things people did to you, but you will never forget how those things made you feel. With Jack, I remember them both.

Eleven.

"She used to be a boy." Or: "He used to be a girl."
This is how many people still refer to transgender
people. By using these phrases, they minimize their
lives.

Being trapped in the wrong body and discovering that
the cage you need to leave is your own skin is like a
war inside your head. Sadly, many people don't make
it any easier for them, especially in Arabic-speaking or
Muslim countries. Fighting with yourself sometimes
and with everyone around you all the time is like
living in hell; some of them survive that torture, and
some others sadly do not—some of them survived the
ordeal of being simply in the wrong place, and others
did not.

In many Arabic-speaking countries, we hear the horror
stories that happened to some of them—including
being killed or committing suicide. In both cases, this

happened because of the outside war—not because of the one within. Every one of them has a story—a unique one. Some turned out to be what many would consider terrible people because of the life they had to endure every single day. They may say, "Don't ask me about what I am, but ask about what I have been through." Many of them had to face loneliness at an early age. They couldn't find any support from their families or anybody around them. "I was so feminine since childhood; my family didn't accept that. They were ashamed to have a son like me, so I left." This is what most transgender people around the Arabic-speaking and Muslim world will tell you at the very start when you ask them about their stories. Many didn't leave their family's house by choice—they were kicked out.

Being different is not easy anywhere—especially when discussing places and cultures with so many rules. It is practically forbidden to be different; some societies denounce you as a sinner. You are doomed to remain an outsider for the rest of your life.

I had the opportunity to witness the journey of some of them who were friends of mine, that journey which started the first time they felt that their gender does not show what they truly are. I had a childhood friend who began to feel that in his second grade. He was attracted to other boys—but not as a boy. He used to show almost everything a girl of that age could show, acting and thinking like one. He would eat a lot to gain weight and wear tight clothes to make his body shape come closer to a female one with hips and breasts.

What he truly wanted to be became more evident during his teenage years. Guys and girls back at school bullied him every day for who he was. He could endure all of that for the sake of a dream he cherished within, a dream of being inside the good body, inside a female body.

You will hear the same story from many of the transgender people around here or perhaps everywhere. They had to go through all this during their teenage years to achieve their dreams.

They all start their physical transformation by taking hormone pills without consulting a doctor. The most popular drug is called Diane. Diane is popular because of its low price and the fact that it doesn't require a doctor's prescription. It also does not help them much as it contains just a little Estrogen. This is why they decide to undergo the surgeries that would make them look like women, such as breast implants, removing Adam's apple, and other plastic surgeries. These surgeries seem to cost much money when you pay in Syrian pounds; for example, a breast implantation costed around half a million, but that was only a thousand dollars before the war. Other plastic surgeries were not expensive either. A nose job costed around a hundred thousand Syrian pounds, about two hundred dollars. That was all before the war in Syria. The dollar was only forty Syrian pounds but increased more than three hundred percent during the war.

To earn money, transgender people used to find jobs

around the country, and the most common jobs they worked at were in makeup and hairdressing. These job opportunities are all gone now because of the war. Currently, most of them are working as prostitutes. Many would tell you how easy it is to do something you love and earn money. That's true, but in this case, sex is what they love, besides how easy it is for them to make money by doing it. Maybe they got arrested sometimes because of that, not because of who they are. When they started to look like women, they would go to any doctor or a psychologist and get a signed report. This report will describe their medical condition and how they were born as a male, but don't feel like one. I read one of those reports once and found the last sentence interesting: "For anyone who reads this medical report, I appreciate your understanding." Appearing as a female, they'd show this report next to their ID as a male when they needed it.

Aleppo was the most popular city for Syrian and Arab transgender people before the war. During the division of the city, some of them would tell you harrowing stories about what happened with their friends on the eastern side of Aleppo after the Islamists entered it; some of them could escape to the western side or to the coastal city of Latakia, where it was safer for them. Others disappeared.

Laila is a transwoman from Aleppo who was trying to escape to Latakia with her transgender best friend in 2013. On their way there, a checkpoint of the Islamist rebels stopped the bus they were on and arrested them the minute they saw their medical reports. They locked Laila and her best friend in the basement of a small building close to that checkpoint. "They put us in a small stinky room down there, and more than fifteen of their men raped us daily", Laila later told me. Everyone raping Laila and her friend went to pray after having sex with them to wipe away their sins. They used to say their boobs kept them alive and were the only reason they didn't kill them.

They were trapped at that place for nearly six weeks,

wishing for death. Laila's boyfriend found them and paid a lot to buy Laila and her best friend out of their captivity. "The day we had our freedom, they came to the room around six in the morning. They shaved our heads and eyebrows and even cut our eyelashes—all while laughing hysterically. Finally, they wrote the word 'heretic' in Arabic on our forehead," she told me.

During the last few years, many have been able to leave Syria, trying to find a better life. For others still there, the cheap plastic surgeries, drugs, or love keep them in the country. Let me tell you just a little bit about what their love life is like. Many will misunderstand the meaning of love a couple of times till they realize that they are used just as sex toys, or in better cases, sex partners for the men they put their trust in.

"Why would he love me, and why would he care about me? No one will marry me or marry any of us— we will never carry their children. Real girls will, and sadly we are not," Heba said. Heba is a transwoman from Homs who left for Turkey, running away from her ex-boyfriend, who used to steal all her escort money and spend it on girls. Heba is one of the most beautiful transgender women you could ever see, and believe me, there were a lot of them around here. Her ex-boyfriend was madly in love with her until he realized she was born a boy. From that moment, all the abuse started. He would abuse her every day, and everyone knew that the cigarette burn marks on her chest were from his hands. Now Heba lives in Turkey, struggling with life and drugs.

Many of the Syrian LGBT community were on the waiting list in Lebanon and Turkey for UN help. At least maybe they had something promising to wait for—not like those still stuck in Syria with no voice. All the international LGBT organizations have only one response to those left behind: "There is nothing we can do as long as you are in a war zone." This was said to me personally. But I still had my voice, which was loud enough.

Some of the transgender people are still stuck in Turkey, and some others left on boats like so many other refugees. They made it to Europe, but sadly, many still live the same life they had in Turkey or Syria—throwing away many chances for a good, respectful life that many of us in Syria didn't even dare to dream about anymore.

My former friend Mo, for example, became a transwoman in Turkey after many plastic surgeries, including breast implants. He lives in Germany now after traveling around Europe for more than a year after buying a fake Greek passport. His rich Arab boyfriend paid four thousand dollars to buy him this passport, according to Mo. At some point, his forged document was stolen by another transwoman who lives in Holland. Mo was forced to ask for asylum in Germany.

His official story was that he had lived in Syria all these years during the war, while in truth, he was in Dubai and later in Turkey. What more could anyone need than being in a place that treats you as a normal human being, a society that treats you based on your actions and how much good you can do—not based on how you look or whom you like to share the bed with. But no, some people like Mo waste every chance to live an everyday life. Mo still has all his old contacts sending him so much money every week. Next to it he still receives social benefits from the German authorities. He speaks excellent German after ten years of being there. When I asked why he didn't have a job, he answered, "Why get one? I am getting so much money for my plastic surgeries." And when I asked him what if the authorities in Germany knew about all this money next to his salary, he said, "They don't dare to mess with me. I am a trans. I can make it sound like a scandal—where they mistreat me for nothing but being trans. I did it once and can do it whenever I want."

Twelve.

I had a few friends whom I met at the start of Elementary School. Most of them turned out to be gay, and that brought us somehow closer. All of us lived in the same neighborhood. My friendship with all of them went off and on through the years. The oldest one I knew was Nour—Nour and I met in the first grade. We were sitting next to each other till suddenly, he started crying, asking to go home. I remember the teacher calling his parents to come to pick him up, and she was whispering that he had pooped in his pants. This story made Nour unforgettable, at least for me as a child.

His wealthy family spoiled him. He was the youngest kid. All his siblings moved out while he was still in middle school— and he never had a good relationship with any of them. Nour lost his dad when we were in the sixth grade. His dad was strict but pampered Nour like crazy. He wrote his will and passed everything he owned on to Nour and Nour's mom. The night his dad passed away, Nour's brother tore the will apart so the whole amount of money wouldn't go only to Nour.

Nour was around twelve when he started calling himself Nour around his friends —a male and female name. At that age, Nour struggled as the most overweight boy around school and in the neighborhood. She had a face full of acne and always wore thick glasses. Nour developed a way of dealing with everything around her, from her controlling mom to how she looked in the eyes of others. She developed a great sense of humor, and she was able to make everyone around her enjoy her company. For me, it was not always humor. She often made fun of herself about who she was and how she looked. She was acting like a clown outside and a broken human inside. Nour always opened up to me in a way she did with nobody else. She found in me the loyal friend she could depend on and tell him anything she was thinking of. I was also the one she feared somehow because I always told her the truth to her face. I always knew she looked up to me as a strong person she could run to when in trouble.

Nour used to have crushes all the time since the age of thirteen. She always called them the "love of my life." I heard this sentence from her more than a thousand times, referring to every guy she put her eyes on. If a man had green eyes, he was *the one*. She had a specific type. He had to be the "man" in bed and hairy. Everything other than that, she would do her best to accept it.

Once, she met a guy online, and they talked only for a few days. It was obvious that this guy was into nothing but sex. Still, he was "the one" for her. They decided to meet, and the plan was he would come pick her up for dinner. She bought new clothes the same day, just for this date. I was at her place while she was getting ready because, as she always said, "I always need you around when I am nervous."

She anxiously waited for him to text her that he had arrived, and she was pacing around, saying, "I pray to

God that he is *the one*. I need love. I have a great feeling about this one. He is the husband and the man of my dreams." I left her place when he arrived, and I saw him from far away sitting inside his car. Let me say one thing. He was nothing compared to what he had described himself to her. I was worried she might be hurt or in a bad mood after this date, but I told myself, "What's the worst that could happen? She won't like him and will return to her game."

That evening, I was meeting another friend for shisha in the gay coffee place. A few hours went by without hearing anything from Nour. Around three in the morning, I got worried. I felt there was something wrong. I called her on her cell. She answered immediately and said with her hilarious laugh between every few words, "Where are you? Why haven't you called me till now?" I said, "I thought maybe you are having a good time with *the one*, so I won't bother you." "*The one,* my ass. He looked and smelled like shit, but I wanted to give him a chance." I interrupted her, asking, "But he has green eyes, right?" She said, giggling, "This is not what you call green eyes on someone's face; these were two spots of shit on someone's face." "So where are you now? Just come, and you can tell us everything here."

She broke in laughing again, "He drove us to a town an hour away from the city and said he had to bring the keys to his friend's apartment. So, he asked me to wait for him at some corner, and that was five hours and fifty-four minutes ago." "Why didn't you call me before? Or why you didn't just take a cab and come back?" "Because I left my wallet at home. I didn't think I would need it, and I have no money charged to call you on my phone."

I took a cab and drove there. When I arrived, I saw that *the one* had left Nour next to the highway. It was an abandoned area where you could hear nothing but dogs barking. When she entered the cab, she laughed like she had just heard the best joke ever. I told her, "If I walked in your shoes, I would never date online here again." She answered, "No, no, it was so fun, like a movie where they dump the hot girl on the road, and then men try to pick her up."

It was not the only time stories like this happened. Once, when Mo and I weren't talking, he called me from an unknown number in the middle of the night, whispering, "It is me, Mo. Please don't hang up. Rami and I were on a date with some straight guys. They picked us up in their car and drove us to the suburbs, around the factories. We got scared because we felt they were planning to harm us. It was only the two of us, and they were a group of four. I got scared when I told them we wanted to go back home, and instead of doing that, the one driving started to speed. We tore open the door and jumped out of the car. They stopped and came back, driving around in circles, trying to find us. I knew you would be the only one who would answer and try to do something—even though we are not talking," So I said, "Enough with all of that. Where are you now?" He whispered, "We are hiding in a swamp. It is a damn sewer; we are squatting in this black water, so they won't find us." I hung up, ran out in my pajamas, and took a cab there, searching for them for an hour or so till I found them. I remember how bad they smelled when they entered the cab. For them, it was an adventure they would laugh about for months.

Nour suffered in one way or another from many of the gays in the scene. Once, Mo borrowed clothes from Nour to wear on a date. But Mo loved those clothes and didn't want to return them. Nour started telling people in the gay scene about that. The story traveled from one gay to another; everyone spiced it up a little. So, it came to Mo's ears that Nour told everyone he had stolen her stuff. That day, I argued with Mo and told him, "You brought this to yourself. Nour lent you the clothes because you begged for them, and now you are not returning them."
Mo freaked out and called all our friends, including Dani, my friend since the fifth grade. Mo told them, *"Emi sharmuta eza bt'hko maa Lucian."* I will never talk with any of you again." *Emi sharmuta* is a Syrian curse in the meaning of: "My mother would be a

whore, if you ever talk to Lucian again." Everyone stopped talking with me, even Dani, whom I had introduced to Mo and everyone else a few months before. And as far as I knew then, Dani couldn't stand Mo.

Eventually, Mo returned Nour's clothes in a nylon bag with Dani. Before they handed over the bag, Mo and another gay guy pissed inside it. That day I met Nour, she was laughing with her eyes filled with tears, saying, "What the fuck is wrong with these people? I thought they would be brothers and sisters." My answer was, "Welcome to being gay here."

I spent that summer with Nour and another gay guy named Safel. It was my twentieth birthday, and I rented an apartment on the beach to celebrate it with my friends. The plan was to enjoy the whole night, cut the cake at midnight, sleep for a few hours, and wake up around sunrise to take cool pictures.

We drank and blew out the candles. Later, we took a

nap to rest a little. When I woke up, none of them was around. I was walking around, wondering where they might be. It was about three thirty in the morning, and I checked the beach from the balcony. There was no one except a group of girls partying, and I knew there was no way Nour and Safel would have joined them because Safel hated women, and he called them *Aakareb* - female scorpions. I went to the kitchen, looked out of the window, and suddenly, I saw Nour and Safel dancing inside an apartment in the beach house facing ours.

I poured a glass of wine and sat at the window, watching them dance with two straight men. When they came back, they feared my reaction. After all, they had left me on my birthday to party with two men from Aleppo. I remember how they sneaked into the apartment whispering. Nour said to Safel, "God, why, my hand is burning like hell! Anyway, we are fucked if Lucian is up and we are not there. It is good that we are on time. God, my hand, you open the door! I need to wash it with cold water." I had pranked them that day by putting chili sauce on the handle of the main entrance of the building and the handle of the apartment's door from outside. I also put a bucket of water above the door. When l opened it, he was wet like a fish. They turned the lights on and saw me sitting with my wine, barely able to breathe out of laughter. We joked about it, and Nour said while giggling, "We deserve it. We deserve it."

At the end of that summer, Nour did a lot to improve herself. She lost weight and borrowed money from me to have her eyes corrected so she wouldn't need the glasses she hated so much. During the winter, Nour became friends with all the people in the gay scene again, and that changed her attitude toward me—by turning into a more confident person. It was the same period when I broke up with Saif and could not stand anyone with an attitude around me. Nour and I lost touch for almost six months, and during this time, she started her real journey.

There was a famous Syrian series called *Aashtar*. It

was about an overweight young girl—wearing thick glasses with bad acne. The grandmom raised Aashtar, who inherited the family's house when the grandmom died. A guy faked his love for the girl till he took the house from her and left her broke and homeless. Aashtar had a gorgeous voice. She got adopted by a big producer who did a makeover for her look and appearance so he could make a big star out of her. Eventually, Aashtar became rich and famous. The guy she loved when she was young came back to her life, took all her money, and destroyed her fame to the point where she lost everything and killed herself.

Nour always joked around, "I am Aashtar. I swear to God I am Aashtar. I will end up like her—we have so much in common." At that time, no one took it seriously, but the longer Nour lived, the more she proved it somehow.

Nour met a guy who always identified himself as straight and nothing but straight. This guy's name was Omar. During that time, Nour had control of all her money and the real estate she inherited from her dad. Nour started spending all her cash on Omar and her gay friends, including Dani, Safel, and even Mo. She bought new phones for some of them and took them to the most expensive restaurants in the city. She rented villas for weekends on the beach or in the mountains during the snow season. She rented an expensive car that Omar always drove and had a bad accident with. Nour had to pay a lot of money to fix the damages.

She was on fire doing everything that came to her head without thinking twice. When she realized she was almost out of cash, Nour decided to do a nose job with the rest of the money. All her friends stopped calling her and cast her out of the group. Omar ignored her calls and messages; she became useless to him. Nour was furious when she heard Omar was seeing a woman who worked as a teacher. She went to this woman's school to pay her a visit and confronted her between classes. "Your damn boyfriend is my husband. Your damn boyfriend used to fuck me in the ass. How can you be with a man like this? He is *gay,* sweetheart." The woman shouted at Nour, "You are a mad person. Don't you dare try to talk to me again!" Nour started screaming. "Listen, everyone! This virtuous teacher is dating my husband, and he is a faggot just like me." Eventually, someone showed up and kicked Nour out of the building.

Nour's mission for revenge was not over with that. She reclaimed all her gifts from her friends so she could sell them, as she was out of cash. At some point, Nour lost everyone around her. She tried to call me, and I ignored her after everything I heard she was doing.

Eventually, she decided to sell one of the apartments she inherited from her dad and sold it for a lower price because she was in a rush to get money again. Omar loved skinny girls, so Nour decided her revenge would work best with some more plastic surgeries. She wanted Omar to regret what he had done to her. She chose to do a Gastrectomy to lose as much weight as possible. The doctor released her from the hospital two days after the surgery and told her to recover at home. He would visit twice a day to check on her. He gave Nour strict instructions on what she could eat and what not. She was allowed only to drink fruit juices and water every two hours and not drink more than twenty-five milliliters every time. She was allowed to walk and move but had to be careful with her stitches.

Nour lasted four days. She went to a shopping mall and smelled the food from one of the restaurants. As she always was, Nour could not stop herself from eating. She went inside, ordered a pizza and a hamburger, and wolfed down both, saying, "What's the worst that could happen? I don't care if I don't lose weight anymore. I only want to eat."

In the evening of the same day, Nour was screaming out of pain, and she was taken to the hospital. When she ate all that food, the stitches in her stomach broke open, and the acid was infiltrating her stomach, harming her other organs. Nour fell into a coma for two weeks and needed three surgeries to save her life.

When Nour woke up from the coma, she asked her mom for me. Eventually, Nour's mom called me and asked me to come to see her. When I entered the room at the hospital, I first noticed the tubes attached to Nour's body, one in her nose and others in her mouth, a few leaving the sides of her tummy and another under her throat. She started crying like a baby, "I am always a bad person when you are not around me. I know I was a bad friend, but you are always the one who's more mature than us. You forgive me, right?"

I started sleeping in the hospital. The last night, she hallucinated and wailed, "I swear to God! I will never do anything bad anymore. I am deformed now. I will have these scars till I die. I don't want to die, not yet. I swear to God. I won't have sex ever again or fall in love with anyone again. I want my family and my friends around me." My heart was breaking hearing all that, so I tried to calm her down and tell her everything would be fine. The following day, she had another leak from her stomach, so she was transferred to Damascus to a bigger hospital, where they put her in a coma for almost a month. Her lungs were failing because of all the surgeries she needed to close the leak.

Nour returned from Damascus, and I remember the first time I saw her after all that had happened. She looked like a skeleton. She could only talk by blocking a small tube with her finger coming out of her jugular notch. Her voice was gravelly, and her skin was so pale.

During the next couple of months, while she was taking the time to recover, she was not improving. Whenever I asked her about that, she answered, "I can't tell you now, but I will tell you everything when I have the good news." I could never figure out what might stop her from recovering after everything she went through and felt because of that tragedy she brought to herself. One day, she called me, and her voice sounded so clear and healthy, which surprised me because I saw her daily. She asked me to come over and have lunch at her place.

When I entered their house, Nour seemed healthy like a horse and talked normally. Everything appeared to be as usual except for her dark scars. I asked, "What's going on? You were acting sick or what?" She burst out laughing, *"Yes!"*. We went to her room, and she started telling me how she sued the doctor who performed the first surgery. She had just won the lawsuit and received compensation. At the same time, she needed to keep herself in this bad shape so she could cancel her military service for being ill and would never be in the condition to serve. I was shocked, but deep inside, I was relieved she canceled her military service because most gay people might not have survived it, at least during the war.

After a few months, Nour started with the same old behavior, so we stopped talking again. During that time, she sold two properties and began to undergo plastic surgeries again. She did another nose job as she found hers ugly on her new skinny face. She did stitches for her lips, which made them look bigger and fuller; she did Botox for her face and chin to get the effect of what the world of plastic surgeries calls "The Nefertiti Effect."

After a year or so, Nour and I started being friends again because she apologized, as always, and I forgave her as I always did. During that time, she planned to leave for Istanbul and then find a way to get to Europe to ask for asylum. At that period, Nour was taking Estrogen shots and birth control pills simultaneously— without a doctor's instructions. She was doing what other transwomen around her did and told her to do. She was surrounding herself with many manipulative people who were telling her anything to get some benefits.

Once, Nour rented a restaurant for a lavish gay party and invited around a hundred people from the scene— and yes, the party took place during the war. Her friends convinced her to throw this party to celebrate that Nour had found a partner; the partner they were talking about was an ex-felon who just wanted Nour's money to leave for Germany. This "partner" never showed up to the party, which was, after all, thrown just for him. Nour was talking on the phone outside with him, and one of the party guests ran to my table and said, "You better check on your friend Nour; she is going crazy." I went outside to check what was happening. I saw Nour banging her head on a streetlamp post and screaming in the middle of the square. I tried to calm her down, but she kept shouting, "I can't see anything, I swear! I can't!" I came closer and held her face with my hands. When I looked into her eyes, I thought she was trying to stage some drama so her "partner" would show up, but her pupils were wide in a weird way. I immediately asked her, "Did you take any drugs during the party?" She said, "No, I did not." I washed her face with cold water, and she calmed down a little. I asked some of her friends who had cars to drive us home, but they refused. "Keep me away from Nour's drama!"

I took a cab and drove her home. Nour immediately disappeared into the kitchen and came to her room holding a bottle of bleach used to clean bathrooms. I was confused but convinced—she just wanted to perform some play, so I would call her guy and tell him what she was about to do. She sat on the bed and started spitting a liquid out of her mouth. She acted like she was drinking the bleach; I stayed calm because I noticed that she spat it out on the dark carpet, and there was no change of color at all. I could tell she put water in her mouth to fake it all. At that moment, I went to her mom's bedroom and knocked on the door. When her mom opened, I told her, "Come to check on Nour, please. Sorry, but I can't deal with him anymore." His mom came, screaming at her son, "You better stop with this drama. Stop making a joke out of yourself."

I left their house and walked home—till now, when I think of that walk, I feel terrified. I took the same roads between home and school for over ten years. In the middle of the way, where I could easily see my apartment, I looked around and asked myself, "Where am I?" I was looking at the street and the building, and I couldn't find out where I was. It was a horrible, terrifying feeling because of the anxiety that Nour always put me through. I always knew that neither she nor anyone in that gay scene was healthy for me, but that night, I realized it was not about being loyal and a good friend for anyone anymore but only for myself for the time being.

Nour later left for Turkey, where her plan was to be smuggled to Europe. She paid three thousand euros for a smuggler who left them waiting for a boat in a forest on the coast somewhere around Izmir. This smuggler never showed up. Afterward, she went to Istanbul, where she stayed with Rami and another friend who both underwent a sex change then.

Nour stayed in Turkey for exactly ten days after wasting around twenty thousand euros for nothing important. Eventually, Nour returned to Syria; Rami mysteriously disappeared after the murder of her transsexual roommate by former escort clients in Turkey. Back in Syria, Nour resumed her same old lifestyle, selling her properties and undergoing more plastic surgeries. After all that work, I saw pictures of her where she looked like a gorgeous real woman.

She decided to try the escape to Europe once again through Turkey, so she sold everything she owned, including her share of her mom's house. This time, the Lebanese didn't let her cross the border to take the flight from Beirut. Nour returned to Syria, rented an expensive apartment, and converted it into a whore house. She acted like the greatest pimp of all time. Less than a month later, she got arrested for enticing minors into prostitution and drug possession. Nour and I hadn't talked for almost two years then. One day, she called me from an unknown number, asking for my help to hire a lawyer. I sold my phone to give her the money to hire one. She sent someone who picked it up. After that, I changed my cellphone number, and we never talked again. During the past years, Nour became a regular in prison.

One might think that Nour ended up killing herself like Aashtar in the Syrian series, but sad enough, she passed away from cancer at the age of 32. People still close to her told me that she was full of regrets. Her last words were, "God rescued me many times after horrible things I've done, but not this time. I ran out of chances and luck; I now seek peace and forgiveness."

Instead of proving all the bullies wrong and using everything she had to reach all her dreams somewhere she could live an everyday life, Nour did nothing but bully herself and make decisions that took her backward instead of going further. Nour was the victim of society, the gay scene, and, most importantly, a victim of herself.

Another victim of all the above was Hani. I have known Hani since the second grade, but we were never close until we were eighteen. He always looked feminine and cute—short, with long blond hair and small green eyes. He had a big butt, a full chest, and no beard. He always looked like a horny teenage girl and acted like one. Hani was always obsessed with sex. The first sexual encounter he had was with one of the neighborhood kids at the age of ten. The first time he did it, he was in much pain. Hani went back home, locked himself in the bedroom, and started to insert different objects into his butthole. He tried everything from cucumbers to small glass bottles. He wanted nothing more than to have sex with this other kid who was twelve. Everyone who was close to Hani knew he had issues, including Hani himself. He always said, "I am jealous of women for having a vagina. All hot men love women because they have two holes. I hate my mom and sister for having a vagina."

Hani was so funny and loving when it came to everyone around him. His family and friends always loved him because he was a giver in every way. Hani is one of the most talented people I have ever met when it comes to being a makeup artist. But instead of taking advantage of his talent, Hani did all this for free for family and friends. He didn't have a job since he finished his military service in February 2011, shortly before the problems in Syria started. He served in an army base around Damascus and considered the service the best time of his life. Hani had sex with more than half of the men in that base, with other soldiers or even officers. He even met the love of his life there, another soldier from Aleppo who had a fiancé. He left his fiancé for Hani, and they were together for almost two years. When Hani finished his military service, he broke up with this guy, telling him, "I am a sex addict, and I won't stop cheating on you. You deserve someone better than me. I don't deserve you. You better return to your life and build a family because you always wanted kids, and I can't give you that." This guy returned to his fiancé, who became his wife later. He named his first child after Hani to honor all the love he had felt for him.

After the war broke out, Hani was always scared that he might be dragged to the service again, so instead of using gay dating apps for sex dates, he started cruising in parks or around other areas where gay men met. Sometimes, he dressed as a woman with a Hijab to have sex with straight men. He would put on full makeup and wear high heels. With the Hijab, he avoided questions about his ID, and it was hiding his

Adam's apple. Like this, he could give blow jobs to half of the hot men in the neighborhood.

Hani never thought about leaving Syria for a place where he could be whatever he wanted. He always said, "I love being here. I can do whatever I want here. I am too stupid to learn a language or live somewhere else." Hani is still living the same life as if all those years had never passed.

Safel is a different case because Safel's family and friends were his victims. Safel was in a relationship with the same guy for almost ten years, off and on. When they met, Safel and I were close. At that time, he was kicked out of home many times and had nowhere to sleep except in my place. During the start of their dating, Safel borrowed so many things from me, from clothes to a watch to money—he never brought any of that back and ignored all of my calls. While he was in Damascus with his boyfriend, he ignored my calls and messages for over six months, so I called his mom to see what was going on. She said,

"I have no idea how you are friends with someone like my son."

It turned out that every time Safel was kicked out of home, he stole stuff from there to sell and spent the money on his boyfriend to show off. He stole so many things from his family, from his sister's gold earrings to his mom's jewelry. While everyone was asleep one night, he even took the TV to sell it. That was precisely what he did with my stuff.

During this period, Safel and his boyfriend had a big fight, which ended with Safel calling the boyfriend's family and his job to tell them that he was gay, which led his boyfriend to be thrown out of home and from work. Later, we stopped talking because of how much he used to stab me in the back. Safel was the friend who had given my family's phone number to Afaf, who had called my mom to tell her that I was gay. Besides playing the ignoring card, I didn't know how to deal with him anymore. I knew he would never do anything but keep lying, so I blocked his number and cut all contact with him, as I always believed that this type of person means nothing but problems, lies, and stabs in the back.

Now, Safel is somewhere in Syria, moving from one place to another because not everyone he stole from and messed with reacted as his family and I did. Eventually, his well-known family removed the last name from him, "We never raised a kid. We raised a wild animal. And now, he is dead to us," They said.

Thirteen.

In 2015, the refugees started reaching Europe. The first person I knew who took on the journey to Europe was someone I knew in my neighborhood. His family had plenty of money, and for them, it was a perfect solution if he would leave the country. He was troubled and abusive, used to hit his dad sometimes, and physically harmed his mom and siblings.

He booked a flight from Syria to Beirut and then another one to Istanbul, where he continued his trip to Izmir. When he arrived there, he was able to contact some people who knew a Turkish smuggler. This troubled guy didn't feel safe taking a regular boat like the other people, who had no other and better options. He got an offer to rent a guide and a Jet-Ski to drive him to the closest Greek island, where he had to pay 4.500 euros. He arrived in Germany after a few days.

I remember hearing this story from one of his close friends at my house. Lara, Dani, and I were listening and looking at each other, puzzled. It sounded so smooth and easy, but there was no way we could raise this amount of money. Lara wanted to try her best to collect money from her relatives abroad. For Dani, this was not an option; a few thousand euros was the price of an apartment in Syria back then.

It was so clear that it was nothing of interest to me, and doing it, even if I could afford it, which I absolutely couldn't, would bring nothing for me except much self-disrespect. For me, breaking any law or crossing borders illegally was a No-go. The idea of living in a foreign country on social welfare as a refugee was just too absurd. I couldn't see myself begging for empathy for everything that happened in my homeland due to war, dirty politics, and international sanctions. I was one of the people who could have taken advantage of this situation because of my homosexuality, but I just couldn't act like a victim. For me, I am a survivor and nothing else. I have always resisted pity because of what I have been through—it's just not fair to assume that I need it. Later, we heard many different stories of people who left Syria; some were terrible and sad, and some were just strange. So many people had to leave because they had nothing left and lost everything. Others just took advantage of the goodness of open-minded European societies.

Rasha's brother traveled to Europe by boat. During his journey, he witnessed a scandal, at least in my eyes. In Syria, we have no black people—when Rasha's brother was on the boat, he started chatting with a group of Africans who spoke English together. He asked them, "Where are you from, guys?" They all looked at each other and answered nervously, "We are from *Sam*." "Sam! Where is that exactly? I never heard of it." "Sam, Sam, the capital of Syria." "You mean *Al-sham*, Damascus." They answered, "Yes, Yes, exactly." He tried to speak Arabic with them, with a Syrian accent, and they were just stunned and had no clue what he was saying. This group of men arrived with him in Germany, and they got accepted as Syrian refugees immediately.

I knew a girl whose boyfriend also reached Europe as a refugee. During his time in Turkey, he had been able to fake Syrian marriage documents to bring his girlfriend later as a "family reunion." The trade-in fake Syrian passports flourished at this time. Such a counterfeit could easily be sold for around 3000 euros. Many who bought them had never been Syrians.

Fourteen.

More and more, young men started to leave mainly to avoid being drafted into military service. The fear of joining the army during the war was overpowering. When I imagined myself in the army, I knew I would have zero chance of surviving because I am incapable of harming anyone, no matter how horrible the people I face are. For me, most of the horrendous people during wars were brainwashed, following orders from their leaders, from bigwigs sitting in fancy offices or five-star hotels, and walking around wearing designer suits.

My strategy to avoid joining the army worked only for a few years—I failed in some classes every semester or even made myself fail a whole year of university sometimes to get extensions for delaying being drafted. The law in Syria then was that you could avoid being drawn into military service as long as you were studying. Things changed later during the war, so my strategy no longer worked. The authorities figured it out, and I could take only two years' extensions for every year of study at the university. During that time, I started feeling scared and increasingly in danger. It was clear the war was not about to end anytime soon. I felt like my future would be quickly wasted.

Besides, I had to struggle with and survive the terrible and worsening conditions of daily life. At that time, I had no paid job nor any savings left, and I was living on some money my parents gave me monthly. Sometimes, I had to spend days without electricity and water. I remember being so hyperactive when the power was on, feeling so happy, like a kid with all the candies in the world. When there was water to shower, it felt like Christmas with many gifts. Did I feel hungry or even thirsty during those times? I did—to the point where I lost counting.

The feeling of walking in a dark tunnel for a long time, where you cannot even see your fingers, is the worst ever. You start to lose contact with reality and hope the light you never saw for ages will not hurt your eyes, forcing you to close them again to protect yourself—once you left that tunnel. I had to walk in deep mud and swim in quicksand. I did it all because I had a healthy relationship with myself. During those times, I started losing it bit by bit because the conditions of my life were stripping the name out of it as *life*—and the shrink inside of me abandoned me and left.

So many people might find me hell of strong, and others might classify me as damn weak, but let me tell you what exactly I am: I am pieces of both above and so much that is still unknown to me. I am a case standing outside of all categories.

My whole life, I had faced uncertainty. It was the first time I honestly dared to ask myself what I truly wanted and wished for. My answer was that I wanted to live normally somewhere else, away from all the bad memories and people. It was the start of summer, and I stood on the balcony of our apartment on the sixth floor at four in the morning, observing the clear, stunning sky, where I could even see a part of our Milky Way. That night, the power was off in whole Syria, so there was no light pollution or even a cloud to hide that we are so tiny compared to the universe. I remember looking down at the street. Every corner was filled with a bad memory; every corner I looked at, I saw myself crying or feeling alone and hurt. And when I closed my eyes, running away from those memories, I saw everything falling apart around me. I remembered the saying, "If you don't like where you are, move! You are not a tree." This was when I realized that I couldn't go anywhere and that I was even more blocked than a tree when it came to moving.

I remember gazing up to the sky, whispering repeatedly, "For whoever is upstairs or whatever can hear me. I have no idea where to go, how to leave, or when to leave. I am exhausted from feeling like a stranger in my own home and around my people. I put all my trust in you." Deep inside, I wanted my inner self to hear of all that before anyone else, and the place for hope that even someone was listening filled the whole world. I suddenly felt unstoppable after tearing my rusted brakes apart and dumping them.

After that, I started checking everything online that could help me, and for almost a year, this stayed my little secret. I shared it with no one, including my mom and dad. Deep inside, I dreamed of moving to Canada to settle there. I always considered it an open-minded country and a place to feel at home, 9000 kilometers away from everything.

I started contacting Gay and LGBTQ organizations around Canada for months, seeking advice or even directions. The answers from those organizations always came with the same sentence: "Sorry! We cannot do anything for you if you are in a war zone."

I thought, "You cannot do anything for me as long as I am in a war zone; then, whom are you helping, and where are you helping?" I remember feeling so disappointed and sad—did that lead me to stop? No, it didn't. I started reaching out to organizations around Europe. Their answers were the same: "We can't help you as long as you are in a war zone." In all my messages to these organizations, I made it clear that I was seeking no direct help. I made it clear that I was reaching out for advice and directions to leave Syria for another country with a legal visa, and nothing but that, so the ones who answered with this were even more disappointing than those who didn't reply at all. I kept receiving those responses till the point where I lost hope. I accepted that it would be my destiny never to be happy and never to move on in my life— and my little secret was buried in the deep ground like it never existed.

I remember talking with people online, where I could act like myself. The closest of those people to me was Thomas from the US, with whom I became close friends. Thomas is one of the most humble, supportive people I ever met. He is simply a *sweetheart*. He always checked on me and cared about me since day one of our friendship and supported me during all that came next. He was not only an amazing friend but also turned into a witness to everything in my life. He and his husband even organized a gathering in their liberal church in Chicago, where he gave me the opportunity to talk via Skype about what was going on in Syria and with queer people. He let me speak in front of the whole congregation. Thomas gave me the chance to let my voice be heard for the first time. He repeatedly taught me what a true friendship meant and what a friend would give no matter how far he was. He showed me in his simple, spontaneous ways how much an act of kindness or words of support can make someone's day and push him further, and never to lose hope.

During that time, I had no friends left around me. Lara moved to Dubai after getting a UAE visa in Lebanon. Hani and Dani always stuck together, and I rarely met them except if they needed something from me or when one of them was fighting with the other. I left my place only once or twice a week. I used to read or watch movies and series to kill time. I remember binge-watching *"Desperate Housewives" and "The Boys in the Band"* because they gave me a feeling of companionship or being a guest at a birthday party in Manhattan. I felt like I was living on *Wisteria Lane,* and all the main characters were my best friends, with whom I felt happy and sad.

Fifteen.

I remember the end of February 2016. I was sick with a pretty heavy flu and could barely move. My brother complained he could not sleep because of my coughing, so he left the apartment and slept at his friend's place for almost a week to avoid getting sick.

I remember the worst night of that week. The electricity was off, and it was freezing cold. I was sitting in the living room in the dim light of a candle, holding my hands above it to get warmth from its flame. I was wearing many thick layers to feel warmer. I remember listening to Rihanna's new album at that time "ANTI," which I was in love with, especially the song "Love on the Brain" and these lines in it, "And it keeps cursing my name. No matter what I do, I am no good without you."

This song described my relationship with myself, my homeland Syria, and so much around me then. It was the time when I felt cursed and nothing but cursed. I remember feeling every step of the time heavy, every single ticking of the clock was so damn loud. I started to muse about many things that had happened and asked myself about the chances of my life changing for the better. My answer was 0,001 percent. It was realistic at the time and in that state of mind. But suddenly, I remembered the central rule in my life: "It is forbidden to give up."

At that moment, I decided to move every zero on the left of that percentage to the right, so my chances of improving my life would become 1000 percent. Guess who came back? The inner shrink had arrived, and all I could say was, "Welcome back, old friend."

That same night, I opened my cell phone and started checking my messages on the only gay social app that I was on. One of the messages was long, and before reading it, the small picture of the sender in the corner of the screen attracted my eyes. Automatically, I pressed on the sender's image and saw this handsome guy with curly hair and a beautiful smile. I started scrolling through his profile to find out more. I read his message, which excited me even more.

He was a Swiss journalist asking me politely if I was open to being interviewed by him about the situation of gay men like me who are trapped in war zones like Syria. I could feel from his message that he was not very optimistic that I would be open to talking about it, and he was worried that some language barriers might be an issue. I told him I would be more than happy to participate in his article. We set a date and exchanged our Skype contacts to talk further.

We Skyped for the first time a week after. His name was Noah. Noah and I started talking when the power was off, my laptop was working on battery, and barely any light was around me. We both felt comfortable. He was a great listener and asked so many intelligent questions. I remember him being surprised by my English skills and that I had agreed to talk with him about the article in the first place. He was also astonished I dared to show my face and identity as a gay man. I opened up pretty quickly to him about so many things because, in the back of my head, I was like, "He is so far away, and he is Swiss, so there's no place for judgment at all." Our chat lasted for hours, and we talked about staying in touch, so we exchanged cell phone numbers. It was mutual respect between us.

The week after our chat, I couldn't stop thinking about him, even with the Great Wall of China I built around my heart through the years. I was never a seeker of love or relationships because my whole life I needed the strength to search for myself between and under the rubble every earthquake in my life had left behind.

I always needed to focus the most on my relationship with myself and not with anyone else. I learned to fall in love with myself, take care of myself, protect myself, and always listen to myself. As with all relationships, mine was never perfect. I was so often mad at myself or found myself ugly —still, I never broke up with myself even once.

I remember that out of the blue, the image of him smiling passed my mind more often, and every time it happened, I tried to push that thought back and said to myself, "Wake up. Stay on the ground, and don't dream away. He is doing his job, and that's it. Besides, who wants to be with someone like me with a miserable life like mine, for God's sake!"

I remember stopping myself from checking his profile. My heart was fragile enough, and I could not afford to have feelings for someone more than 3.600 kilometers away.

A couple of weeks later, I got a message from him, asking how I was doing. I replied to him, and we chatted shortly and decided to Skype again soon. After a few days, he found some free time for me when I had electricity. We started to talk less formally, like any two people who met online. I was telling him about friends and about the gay scene in my city—he was very interested, so he kept asking questions, and I was always answering. We chatted that day for over three hours, and I started to like him as a good friend. I just loved his personality and how educated and cosmopolitan he was.

During that time, I was still in touch with Nour occasionally, depending on her shape. She called me after midnight, asking me to come to her place for wine because she missed me. When I told her I was not feeling that well and not in the mood to hear her friends' dramas, she said, "Speaking of them—you better come so I can tell you what the trend is to cancel the military service." Immediately, she aroused my curiosity, so I got ready and was at her place in less than ten minutes.

Being dragged to the military service was the monster hunting most of the guys around, particularly gay men. Nour started telling me about the new trend in the scene to eliminate this monster. Gay men would dress as women, act like them, and wear tons of makeup. Then, they would visit one of the known psychologists and talk with him about being trapped in a man's body. He would then write a medical report with his signature and an official stamp. The report would state that these men feel like women and are, therefore, not a fit for the service in times of war. Armed with this medical report, the men would go to their military service office and hand it out there with a request to get the opportunity to be checked by the highest medical board in the military. When this board would find them unfit, it would write this short sentence in the military book: "He was exempt from military service for medical reasons."

This sentence was all anyone needed. It was a one-way

ticket to freedom. Nour told me about a few people I knew who had done it already. It became a kind of competition to see how they would enter the room of the military medical board and what dress and makeup they would wear. One of the queers had done it a few days before, and he went to meet the board after renting a red wedding dress with a three-meter red chiffon train. He entered the office like a bride on her wedding day. The doctors were shocked, dazzled and amused at the same time. One of them asked him about his name, and he answered with a female name instead of his real one, and that was it. They wrote the magic sentence in his military book, and he was free to go.

Nour insisted on calling another guy who was still in the process and asking him to come over so that he could tell me everything in person. I knew him from before, and I was pretty surprised. He was masculine, with so much hair on his shoulders and a long black beard. He was a bear. When he came over, he looked a little different. He told me he was asked to be checked more than once by the medical board because they were not convinced; he was not just faking it to avoid his service. Even though he had shaved his beard, wore tight clothes, and put some makeup on his face, their assessment would not be changed.

When I asked him what exactly his plan was for the next time, he said he had been taking shots of Estrogen for a week and would keep taking them until his next appointment at the medical board. I felt I should consider the plan seriously when I heard these stories. I knew my chances would be low because of my beard and body shape, but on the other hand, I had long, curly hair and a skinny physique. I decided it could be manageable. No matter what, I had to try so I wouldn't regret it and blame myself later. I wouldn't take any Estrogen shots and would do nothing that would leave permanent marks on my body.

During that time, I talked with Noah about it. I told him the whole story. His opinion was exactly like mine. Nour made an appointment for me to see one of the psychologists who was a member of the highest medical board in the military. The meeting was scheduled for eleven in the morning, and the plan was that I would be at Nour's place at six in the morning. When I arrived at Nour's home and entered her bedroom, I saw a pile of makeup and girl's clothes on her bed waiting for me. She had invited some friends to help with my makeover. I stood there bemused, and Nour grinned, "Finally, my dream is coming true; you will be one of us now."

First, I had to shave my beard. I looked like a washed Chihuahua without it. The next step was to add some extensions to my natural hair and eventually came the makeup. Everything went fine while sitting on a chair with six hands on my face and in my hair. At some point, when the time for the cheap mascara came, and they put it on my eyelashes, my eyes started tearing like the eyes of a mother who had just buried her children. They turned red, and the tearing did not stop. I ran to the mirror to wipe that mascara off. Everyone shouted and screamed, "You can't check the mirror now! The makeover is still in process!" "You are kidding me! I am about to go blind!"

When I stood in front of the mirror, I burst into laughter. What I saw was not someone who looked like a girl. I looked like a zombie in drag. Everyone was laughing, but we had to go back to work as we ran out of time. I washed my face and added some foundation, powder, and lipstick. Nour's verdict was without a doubt: "You look like a lesbian who's trying to join the military. This isn't what we call makeup. You should look like a cheap whore to make it realistic." When the time came for the clothes, I couldn't listen to any of them. They wanted me to dress like a prostitute. Instead, I just put on tight clothes and oversized sunglasses of mine.

In the cab, Nour taught me to speak like a girl, which was impossible for me to do. On the way to the doctor, a police checkpoint stopped the car. It was a Friday, and sometimes Fridays brought with them some troubles after the prayers. When they stopped us, I froze. I was so scared they might notice my makeup or something else. Lucky for me, they checked randomly and asked only for the cab driver's license.

When we arrived at the doctor's building, Nour insisted on refreshing my lipstick, and while doing that, a group of teenagers noticed us and started shouting in the middle of the street, "*Tantat! Tantat!*" – "Fags!". I wanted to shut them up, but then I remembered how I looked. Did that stop me from confronting them? Of course, it did not. I told them if they didn't shut up, I would pay them a visit at school and tell all their friends that they were just like us. I remember how they gaped at me, more scared of how I looked than of my threats. They just walked off without saying another word.

In front of the doctor's door, I started shaking like a freezing puppy—I was so nervous. What the hell was I doing here? What if someone I know or someone who knows my parents recognized me? I pulled myself together and asked Nour to come inside with me. But she refused, "Hell no! I can't do that." When the time came, I entered and spoke to the doctor in a low voice while stopping myself from laughing. He started asking me questions like, "What are you doing here? How can I help you? What are you feeling right now?"

When he asked all that, I turned mute, and I started looking at the floor and the ceiling. He was confused about why I was not saying anything, so he called Nour and asked her to join us. Nour winked at me and whispered, "You want to cancel your service with being a fag, or are you trying to be sent to a mental hospital?" I couldn't stop laughing, so the doctor said, "Here we go! Someone is alive and smiling. Tell me, son, how can I help you? Don't be shy. You can tell me anything, literally anything." Nour looked at me and noticed that I was struggling to make my voice softer, so she put her hand on my knee and started talking with the doctor nonstop like she had just swallowed a radio while airing the news.

She told him I had tried to kill myself twice because I

felt trapped in the wrong body. After thirty minutes of Nour inventing stories about me and my dream to become a woman, the doctor interrupted her torrent of words, "There's no need to hear more, son." He gave us the report with his stamp and signature and asked Nour to wait outside so he could have a word with me.

When Nour left the office and the door was closed, the doctor stood up, sat beside me, and said, "Look, son. There must be another way to avoid military service. If you are gay, it doesn't mean you have to be a woman. Don't fight whomever you are inside. Try to leave to a place where they will appreciate you like everyone else—by the way, you are a bad liar, so stay like that. Nowadays, it is refreshing to meet someone like you."

I immediately told Nour, "Fuck it, I won't do this anymore. I just cannot." Nour was going crazy the whole time on the way back home, "I feel sad for all the makeup you wasted. I thought finally you would become one of us. We could become trans together." I was laughing while I removed the makeup on my face.

The old cab driver observed Nour and me, confused about what we might be, women or men.

Noah and I started talking more often in the coming period, once or twice every two weeks.

At the end of May 2016, eight bombings were carried out by ISIS in the cities of Jableh and Tartus on the coast. 184 people were killed, and at least two hundred left injured. In Jableh, the terror attack targeted the hospital and the central bus station. Many doctors and nurses were among the victims. In this bombing, three kids I was teaching English were killed. They died with their mom, who worked in that hospital as a nurse. The three kids were eleven, ten, and nine. They had escaped from eastern Aleppo to find a better and safer place with their parents.

When I got the news, Noah texted me fifteen minutes later to check on me. I was struck by one of my strongest breakdowns ever. I remember talking with Noah and crying the whole time on the phone. It meant the entire world to me that there was someone to talk to after that horrible news. During the next few weeks, I fell into an awful depression. My hate and disgust could drown the whole world. During all this time, Noah was by my side. We talked almost daily while he was in New York for a business trip. With time, Noah and I became closer and closer to a point where we could easily call each other best friends. If it was not because of him, maybe that depression would have led to something tragic.

We started talking almost daily on Skype and discussed everything: love, friendships, history, politics. At that time, Noah encouraged me to write my story down—from the bad to the good because, in his eyes, I was not a victim but a hell of a survivor. This touched me so profoundly because this was precisely how I wished to be seen through everything I pulled myself out of, as healthy as possible. If it was not because of Noah—this book may never have existed, and my story would never have been told; perhaps my story could have been forgotten even by me because, as humans, we use oblivion as a weapon to survive. Noah convinced me that my story should be told and never be hidden and reminded me in his way how strong I could be and always will be.

I remember staying up the whole night, struggling to put my memories into words, trying to write my story under the light of a candle. The following day, and before sleeping for a few hours, I texted Noah I had written a little and would read it for him. With time, I started diving deeper and deeper into my writing. I started learning to be stripped of any facade I had built around my soul, only in front of him. If I were to tell the sea how Noah made me feel, the sea itself would leave its shores, its shells, and its creatures and follow me to get a glance of Noah. For the first time in my whole life, I felt I had always searched for a homeland and had somehow discovered it.

The idea of telling Noah how I felt about him was something I had never experienced before. It felt like tasting ice and fire at the same time. I think this is what's called *love*. I remember Nour asking me why I always seemed absent. "I think I have feelings for a guy I am talking with from Switzerland," I said. I will never forget Nour's answer. "You are the full package. You are smart, handsome, loyal, and kind. But you are Syrian, which means you are cursed. No one can see the good in us anymore; they are blinded by what they see daily on the news." I agreed, but deep inside, I felt that I should put my pride aside for once in my life and tell Noah because it was also his right to know all of that, and my feelings for him were strong enough to a point where I couldn't steal this from him.

We talked almost every day so I could read to him what I had written, but once a week, we drank wine together on Skype. I waited until that night to gather the courage to admit my feelings toward him—the Syrian wine would help. While processing all that I wanted to say to him, and before admitting it all, I remember glancing at my phone and seeing a notification from the gay dating app we met on. I looked back to my laptop screen to see Noah's face—

without thinking twice, I was sure I wanted Noah and only Noah. I remember holding my phone in my hand and deleting my account and the app in a few seconds. He was still talking when I asked him my famous question, "Can I say something?" And he replied, "Yes, sure, you can say anything." "You are sure I can say anything? Because what I am about to say is something I never said to someone before, and I am hell of scared of your reaction, but I have nothing to lose if I tell you, while I might lose a lot if I don't."

Noah paused a few seconds and said, "You can tell me everything. What's between us is bigger than this introduction." "What exactly is between us? I could do this by texting you, but I feel safe enough to tell you this right here. I understand if you need to collect your thoughts about this because I already did, and I am sure of my feelings." Noah got nervous. "What's going on?" I stuttered and answered him, "I am sure I have feelings for you. Here I said it, and there's no need to say anything about it now." He kept silent for a few seconds, and it felt way longer to me; then he sighed, smiled, and said, "I have had these feelings for a while, too, but I kept them for myself. I never wanted to bring it all up while you are going through so much."

At that moment, I felt like floating in the skies, riding a small, fast white cloud that could carry me anywhere on Earth. Trust me, I wanted to fly nowhere but to touch Noah and kiss him. For the first time, I could forget about all the sadness inside me. I was so scared of the unknown and what might happen next, but I needed to enjoy the moment, and I did. It was a turning point in my life.

Growing up and learning about love in life, I remember listening to the song "Jolene" by Dolly Parton for the first time when I was around thirteen years old. Through the years, this song opened my eyes to something: even in relationships based on love, someone might reject the other at some point because of another person or for different reasons. Somehow, this song made me overthink being rejected by someone I like or even someone I could love and have loved me back at some point. Repeating in my head the idea of being rejected stopped me from saying or admitting so many things in my life. Still, not with Noah; he always made me feel safe beyond imagination—without even a touch or any intimacy between us.

For the next few weeks, we talked every night before bed until the other life-changing day, when we said to each other, "*I love you.*" We decided to face the unknown together, no matter what.

Sixteen.

We developed a plan to meet. As a start, I had to renew my passport, which was about to expire around the beginning of the new year. If you are a guy around my age in Syria and have at least one brother, it is mandatory to do military service. Many men studying at university, like me, could get an extension of two years for every year of study. I was around twenty-five years old and starting my graduation year. Under the law in Syria, I could get a two-year extension to graduate. I remember going to the military service office in my city to ask about the papers and the procedures I had to go through for the renewal of my passport. After waiting for four hours outside to be allowed to enter the building and ask my few questions, one of the bitchy employees told me that her colleague, who oversaw these papers, had a couple of days off and that I should come back next week.

When I returned after a week, the woman in charge of the papers bluntly announced that I couldn't get my new passport. "Did you pay the bail money?" she asked. I answered, "No, what bail are you talking about?" "This bail is a payment that will be gone if you don't get extensions from military service by a Syrian embassy abroad before your extension from here is over." This bail amounted to 300 US dollars, next to other fees, making the Syrian passport the most expensive one in the world with a price of 800 US dollars, while I couldn't travel anywhere with it. At that time, 300 US dollars corresponded to about 200,000 Syrian pounds. A couple of years earlier, this money could have been the first payment to buy a gorgeous apartment on the beach.

After collecting the money by selling some stuff and raising some from here and there, I had to go to the bank, which took the money from me and handed me in return a piece of paper to prove it had been paid. I remember running back to the military service office with that paper. On the way, I sent videos to Noah telling him that I was so happy to be over with this after almost a month. The bitchy woman started preparing the document and signing it; when she discovered that my previous extension had not been noted on my file because another employee forgot to transfer it from the computer system there. As a result, my name was registered at every border crossing in Syria and at the military police that tracks and arrests anyone who is avoiding the service.

I couldn't believe my ears for a few seconds and said, "This is impossible. How could a mistake like this happen? What about my graduation year? So, I could be arrested right now, taken, and drafted to the military service, and till someone realizes this mistake, I would be dead." She looked at me and said in a snide tone, "It is not my mistake. Go ask them to fix it. All I am certain of is that I can't issue the document." I went to the other office to tell them about what happened. They couldn't care less, "Why are you crying? What if you go to the military? Are you not ashamed of yourself? You are a man, aren't you? Men don't cry."

I was afraid I could be arrested because of this mistake, and I could not even tell Noah. That was my biggest fear at that moment. I left that office and went to the highest officer in charge of the whole station. After thirty minutes of waiting, I was allowed to enter and talk with him; I told him the entire story, and all he got to say was, "Go back to that office and tell them to send a request to cancel your name from the list." After I did as I was told, all the women in that office suddenly behaved like lambs. "Yes, sure, we will do it immediately. Just return in ten days to get the paper for your passport."

On my way home, I felt I couldn't breathe anymore. I remember being scared to tell Noah. I didn't want to worry him. I texted him that I needed to talk with him immediately. He called me, knowing that there was something wrong. I tried to stay calm and tell him everything slowly, but the second I heard his voice, I fell apart and started crying again—I just felt damn cursed.

We hear this sentence from many people: "It is all going to be fine." This sentence had never touched me before, and it used to enter my head from one ear to leave from the other right away like a cartwheeling cigarette butt. Still, when Noah said it, he colored my world again; I couldn't do anything but believe him, and what's better than always trusting someone who will do everything he can to make you feel safe?

I couldn't wait ten days, as they asked me to. I had no trust in those people, gossiping and drinking coffee and Mate tea all day at work at their desks. No one was in the office except two employees when I arrived there. When I asked about my paper, they said, "Oh, we forgot about it. We will do it right away." I was shocked and couldn't do anything; I thought they wanted me to bribe them with some money to get it done, but a part of me was refusing that. Not only because of how wrong it was but also because I didn't know how to do it.

I started digging about the woman who was responsible for this mistake in the first place so I could tell her what was happening. Maybe she would feel guilty and ask her colleagues to fix it as soon as possible. After letting them trash her by calling her name and asking where exactly she was working, I went early the next day to another building to her office. When I entered, I told her I might lose my entire future because of this and that time was running out.

I still see the nasty look on her face while she was chewing an apple and asking, "Why is it my mistake? I don't believe it is my mistake as I no longer work there. I won't take any responsibility for this. Things like this always happen." I answered, "I don't care who did this! All I care about is the mistake to be fixed!" She stared at me, miffed. "Go out of my face. I don't want to see yours anymore. What's the big deal if you go to the army—you won't be the first one to go and die there and certainly not the last."

I didn't dare to say another word to her because she could call security from the military police. I said, "Thanks for your time," and left. Weeks and months passed before anything even changed in my procedure. In February, I had to do my first semester exams during all the chaos in my life.

The day before the last exam, new laws canceled the possibility of issuing extensions to graduate. Now, I was officially a runner from the service. My studying extension was only valid till the middle of March. I remember attending my last exam without any sleep. I went there, trying not to think of what might happen next. This didn't work out. I passed out in the middle of the exam hall, and when I regained consciousness, I insisted on continuing even with the thirty minutes left.

I passed the exam with pretty good grades. I remember leaving that exam hall scared to look back because deep inside, I knew it might be the last exam I would do, and I would never be able to graduate, and I would leave without any university degree.

I grew up in a family where education or degrees were almost worshipped. I knew this was another thing that would make me inferior compared to everyone else around me. If I had had some contacts or was from a wealthy or powerful family, all that could never have happened to me. They didn't want to do their jobs, and I had no one to fix it. Even remembering this makes me feel bad sometimes—to the point that it distracts me from reminding myself where I am now. Around that time, I finally got my passport after more than four months, and it was a celebration for Noah and me, as our first victory together.

When March arrived, my parents were trying to get me another extension to graduate. They wouldn't accept the idea that I would leave without any university degree. During that time, Noah researched destinations I could go to as Syrian; there were not so many, but even for those few, Syrian citizens had to undergo entirely different procedures. We even considered a refuge for me in Malaysia, Ecuador, or Sudan. Still, my parents and my brother were trying to find someone in Lebanon to sponsor me for a maximum stay of one year there. My mom is half-Lebanese, and her half-sister also, and this half-sister has Italian citizenship aside.

My brother tried to organize someone through her to sponsor me in Lebanon with money. Eventually, he found Mirvat, a close friend and a neighbor of my half-aunt, who agreed to sponsor me for two thousand dollars. No one of us had this amount of money, but my brother managed to get it from a friend of his who lived and worked in Lebanon. This contact would pay the money to Mirvat.

After Mirvat received the money from my brother's friend, she began to act as if something unfortunate had happened with the sponsorship and that it would be difficult for her to sponsor me. She started ignoring all the messages and calls from my brother and his friend. Eventually, she texted my brother back. Her husband had found out about the sponsorship and threatened her with a divorce if she went further with it.

During that time, my parents could only get me an extension from military service for four months. This left me only two options: the first was to leave Syria without passing my last semester's exams to graduate, which meant that I would lose all the years I studied at university, or I would stay in Syria, graduate, and be stuck in a void for the rest of my life while trying to avoid the military service.

I started questioning myself about whether I felt at home in Syria. The answer was: No, I barely did. Don't get me wrong. I worship Syria, but what we love does not always love us back. This is how I described my relationship status with the place where I grew up. It was the first time I admitted that I loved Syria, but she never loved me back. And I loved its people, but sadly, they never loved me back. My life in Syria was never even close to being described as easy, even before the war. This huge confession deep down led me to another confession—that my home is a person who lived so far away. This person was Noah, and it was the first time I confessed that Noah is my home, a home that I love and that loves me back for nothing other than being myself.

The idea of leaving to Lebanon became more real between Noah and me. Time was running out because my extension was about to expire in a month. If I couldn't find a way to leave Syria, my survival chances would be diminished. At that time, I was powerless, and the me who was born with a body armor on started being simply a crushed moving entity. The bad luck, the fear, the many bad memories, being away from whom I love, losing my chances to graduate university, the deprivation, and not being able to use water whenever I needed it or even eat whatever I wanted—all of that made my many old scars grow against nature to become open infected wounds. I turned into a person who feared even the simplest things to do, and overthinking became my addiction. The only thing that stopped me from harming myself was the sense of not being alone—Noah was present in every aspect of my life, even with the three thousand six hundred kilometers between us. I could sleep only after I had talked with Noah. I looked forward to waking up only to see him, and I kept going in my daily life only because of Noah. We added each other on a location share app. I felt safe because I knew he could follow where I was.

At that time, my friend Dani and I made plans to leave together to Lebanon, and I was happy somehow with that plan because it would feel better being in a foreign country with someone I had known since the fifth grade, even if I didn't trust him much. That plan had been discussed between us with details since the start of the summer, and it was the first time I felt that he was determined about something.

When that summer ended, Dani disappeared for almost ten days. He was not contacting me in any way or answering my calls. I could feel that something had come up, and I was right. One evening, he knocked on my door and just announced, "I need to use the bathroom." When he returned, he went directly to the kitchen, where he prepared a shisha for himself while I was talking with Noah on the phone. After I hung up, he came with the shisha, sat down on the sofa next to me, and said with a smirk, "Ah, I forgot to tell you the big news, or maybe you already heard about it. I'm leaving for Erbil in Iraq in two weeks." Our Lebanon plan was dead, and we never talked about it again. I was stunned for a couple of seconds, and then I remembered who Dani was, so my disappointment faded immediately. In fact, I was happy that he could leave Syria for a place he might find better than where we already were.

During the following weeks, I helped him with everything from buying things he needed to packing his luggage. I remember the day he left for Damascus to fly to Erbil and how much I cried. Our lives were falling apart. We would all be scattered around the world. More than thirty people from Dani's family and friends gathered at his place to say their goodbyes.

After Dani left, I became even lonelier. I spent my days at home without leaving—even for a short walk. I was running out of time with my extension day after day, and the fear in Noah and me grew bigger and bigger. The idea of me being stuck in Syria could kill any chance of us being together. How unfair it was to Noah to be with someone with a miserable life like mine. If I truly loved him, I should let him go to be happy with someone who doesn't live in a cursed land like mine, cursed by making everyone rip pieces out of its wings, a land that was cursed because many of its own people sold it cheap and destroyed it.

Noah and I always talked about everything and discussed all our options. Every time I brought up the topic that all the misery in my life was not fair for him, his answer used to be, "Everything is going to be alright. We will find a solution like we always do. I am with you because I want that and won't go anywhere."

Our worst-case scenario was to meet in Lebanon. But Lebanon wasn't easy at all. The authorities there requested a hotel reservation and to show one thousand dollars in cash on the Lebanese side of the border. But, of course, nothing was certain. The real authority here was the officer's mood at the border crossing. Nour once had a five-star hotel reservation and even showed the dollars. They denied entry. We knew if we would do it this way, we had to prepare ourselves for many unpredictable hurdles.

During the last week of my extension, Mirvat, who had taken two thousand dollars to sponsor me on papers, started answering my brother again after he had asked her to pay back the money because she had done nothing at all. She told my brother I should try to come to Lebanon to wrap up the sponsorship.

Twenty-four hours before my extension ended, my brother came home in a hurry and knocked on my bedroom door. It was around noon, and he told me hastily I had to leave Syria before tomorrow morning, or I would be stuck. I should take a minibus to Damascus and then cross the Al Msnaa border because none of the other border crossings between Syria and Lebanon would allow Syrians to enter. Mirvat would contact me the second I arrived in Lebanon to pick me up.

His words formed a vast cloud pouring down nothing but fear and nervousness. I called Noah the second my brother stopped talking to tell him everything. I remember how anxious he was about me when he heard this plan but did not show it. I had to call my parents right away to see them and say goodbye to them. After less than an hour, my mom, my sister, and my little niece opened the apartment door. My mom hugged me immediately and started crying. We were both shocked that everything was suddenly happening so fast. For a few minutes, I thought my dad was right behind them on the staircase. I asked, "Where is Baba?" "Your dad is not coming; he was hiding his tears on the way here. He stopped the car on the side of the road and left. His heart couldn't handle saying goodbye or even hugging you. Maybe it's the last time, he said. He is my little one, and I can't let him leave and see him going far away from us. He couldn't do it."

It killed me hearing this, but deep inside, I understood what he was saying and how hard it might be to say farewell to your loved ones. I remember my niece crying because she wanted to play at the park, so my sister left with her. I was alone with my mom for a couple of hours. We drank coffee and smoked like we always did. My mom tried to dissuade me from the plan of leaving Syria. They would never let me go to the military service nor let anything bad happen to me; she said, "What will happen to me and your dad when you leave? You are the best we created, and now you are just flying away!"

I stayed determined. I wanted nothing but to be with Noah, so I told her, "If you love me, you must let me go. There's not even one reason left for me to stay and to be punished for nothing but being myself. If I don't leave now, I won't leave ever. Everything that happened to me and is still happening is letting me rot alive." Deep inside, I did not doubt that I was already in pieces, but soon, I might be able to put all my pieces back together — in the shape and the colors I wanted them to be.

When I finished talking, my mom answered, "You really want to leave and be a stranger, nothing but a stranger your whole life?" Until now, whenever I face difficulties in life, I hear my mom's voice saying this sentence. It hurts a lot every time I remember it, but I am trying my best to prove her wrong. My mom felt guilty that she said it, but she wanted to use some tough love to keep her little one always around.

My mom insisted on staying till I leave, but I couldn't let her do that. I knew she couldn't handle seeing me leaving for a life far away from her. Nor could I. I was worried she would retreat to my old room, start smelling my clothes, and look at pictures from my childhood. These thoughts were heartbreaking enough to ask her to return to the village and be with my dad. She left the apartment after we both cried again with long hugs. I couldn't imagine this world without my mom; until now, I simply can't.

After my mom had left, Noah and I discussed the details. He had tried to use some of his contacts to suggest places we could rent in Beirut—where it would be safe for both of us. A friend of Noah's in

New York had contacted a Palestinian guy who grew up in Lebanon so Noah could get in touch with him; this guy had organized a charity event for Syrian gay refugees a couple of weeks earlier. The guests, drinking their champagne all night, got free t-shirts with "*Mr. Gay Syria*" printed on them as a giveaway. We were confident he might give us some directions. When this guy heard that Noah was a Swiss journalist who needed some advice, he didn't hesitate to talk to him. Noah gave him an account of the situation, asking for leads. This guy, who had collected maybe thousands of dollars from New Yorkers fit for generosity, left the conversation without any answer when he knew that I was Syrian.

The only solution left to us was a temporary one. Noah booked a hotel for me in Beirut online. I had to run and print the reservation on paper to show it later at the border crossing. When I came home, it was around eight, and I still had to pack a small backpack with only some clothes and a carryall where I stowed my Syrian documents, which were already translated into

English and German. I remember how heavy my head felt and how I dealt with everything like a robot. Somehow, my emotions were shut down, and I had no strength to think about what might happen next. I knew there could lie ahead bad scenarios for me. I could be stopped on the road to Damascus at a checkpoint where they would realize my extension would be over in a few hours. Or the Syrian border officers wouldn't let me leave the country, or the Lebanese wouldn't let me enter Lebanon because they didn't have their morning coffee yet. The safest thing for my soul was shutting my brain and emotions down.

Around ten at night, Noah asked me to rest, which I tried to do. The second I was about to fall asleep, my mom called and told me she was downstairs to see me again. I remember walking down the stairs slowly, one step and one floor after another, trying to delay saying goodbye to my mom. She was leaning on my sister's car with no strength to stand on her feet. I remember her saying with eyes full of tears how much she loves me and wants nothing but to see me happy and safe. I remember the last time I hugged my mom, the comforting scent of her perfume, and how sweet her hair smelled. I remember her soft, silky cheeks touching my face while kissing goodbye. I stopped myself from crying in front of her; I knew there were people around us in the street who had bullied me in the old days. I wanted to show my mom that I was damn strong. That I could endure everything, and she had raised a lion. I remember laughing and joking with her to prove I could handle everything with hope. My little niece, barely walking or speaking, hugged my leg. She couldn't understand anything but could sense farewell emotions.

I knew I should memorize every image of my mom because she was not the one to be forgotten. The picture of all of them waving for me and my mom's sparkling eyes in the mirror faded away the farther they drove. I remember the second the car turned to the left and disappeared at the end of the street. My eyes became like an abundant spring from sadness.

I rushed back upstairs to the apartment and went to bed, trying to sleep. Every time I forced my eyes to be closed, they opened again without control. A part of me wanted to scan my room to remember every tiny detail. I started scanning the walls and the furniture, staring at every poster I had once pinned on the walls, remembering all the things or the songs that made me hang these pictures of these famous people and how much all of them inspired me in one way or another to be who I was. I retained every corner of that room that I cried or laughed in.

I pulled myself together to get ready. My brother entered my room, complaining about how I was dressed. His problem was my red leather handbag because he worried anyone might bother me on the way or at the border. Of course, I didn't listen to him; I never hated anything more than someone telling me how to dress.

I left the house with my brother and his friend, who wanted to drive me to the bus station. Before leaving that apartment, I turned back. In our living room stood a small statue of Holy Mary, and I always had an indescribable relationship with her. I was never into religion or following anything or anyone. Still, Holy Mary is simply holy for me, maybe because she is a mom, and I love my mom so much. If my mom couldn't protect me from something bad, I was convinced Holy Mary would. I always had placed a rounded metal icon of Holy Mary under my pillow. I had put it in my handbag before anything else.

Before leaving the place where I had spent all my life in Syria, I needed to stand in front of Holy Mary to ask her to watch out for me. I remember kissing her forehead and shutting the door without even looking back.

I had to talk with Noah at the bus station to feel less scared and nervous. I needed to hear his voice before going toward the unknown. I can't remember exactly how many times we said "I love you" on that last call. We both knew I couldn't speak English with all the people around me on the bus. And we knew my Syrian cell phone number wouldn't work once I entered Lebanon.

I had to hang up, even though I needed him even more when I saw that small black bus crammed with people. Everything happened so fast that I just said goodbye to my brother without hugging one another. I found a narrow seat in the last row between two men. When the bus left, the choking feeling of loneliness overwhelmed me. I cried silently, hiding my warm tears while leaving my old city. It was after one in the morning, and the streets were empty. I remembered the bad and the good on every corner we drove by.

I hadn't slept for almost twenty-four hours. I had to stay awake in case something went wrong. After some time, we drove toward Homs, where the war had raged. A military checkpoint stopped the bus to check people's IDs; I was worried they might ask for my military book and see that my extension was about to be over that day. I remember breathing slowly to calm myself down. Suddenly, the bus driver looked back at everyone and announced, "Hey everyone, they want to check all the military books." I handed the officers mine with a confident smile while my legs trembled like a sewing machine. In less than a minute, they returned the documents and wished us a safe trip, but that sudden rush of adrenalin kept me even more awake.

On the way to Damascus, the bus left the highway and took a small, dark road. Everyone around me grew nervous. Kidnappings were common at that time. A young woman was sitting next to an old man. She asked the driver firmly, "Why are you driving here? This is not the main road!" The driver told her he was picking up his mother-in-law. We all were, of course, not convinced. While everyone was gawking through the windows into the pitch-dark night outside and then through the bus's windshield, an old lady just showed up in the spotlights, waiting with some bags. Everyone sighed in relief. The whole road to Damascus, the old lady and the young woman joked about how everyone

thought we were about to be kidnapped, how safe
Syria once was, and how scary it is nowadays.

The suburbs of Damascus unfolded a landscape of
ruins. Whole neighborhoods were wiped out, and two
people in front of me discussed the apocalyptic
scenery, how Damascus was cut off from water for
months, and how hundreds of missiles were shot daily.
But amidst all the destruction, I could understand why
so many people fell in love with Damascus again—the
moment we reached downtown. It felt like ages since I
had visited the capital last time, while just five years
had passed.

The bus driver asked for my name, and I replied,
surprised, "It is me. Why?" He said I should leave the
bus here, and my brother's friend would pick me up. I
was standing in a neighborhood I'd never been in,
waiting for someone to show up. I called my brother to
check with him, and he told me that maybe his friend
might still be asleep, which was true. I took a cab to

his place.

When I arrived, I chatted with the sleepy friend until the driver who would bring me to the Lebanese border picked me up. My brother's friend didn't move at all and just said, "Just go! You will be fine."

The driver asked for a hundred dollars for the 30-minute trip to Lebanon. He would hand me a thousand dollars, which he always kept in the glove box for occasions like this to show to the Lebanese officers. Once they had let me enter, I would pay him. After we had talked things through, I sent Noah a recording message that I was heading to the borders now and would call him the second I had Wi-Fi.

During the short ride, my driver made dozens of phone calls to different people. I had a chance to take a picture of him and send it to my brother and Noah. I had no idea why I did it exactly, but it made me feel safer because I had no trust in anyone. When the driver finished all his calls, he glanced at me and asked, "Do you have a white shirt in your bags?" "Yes, I do. Why?" "Because the Lebanese officers won't let you enter if you wear a T-shirt." "It is thirty-two degrees outside. What should I wear, a suit?" "You are like my son, and I have done this for more than fifteen years on this road between Damascus and Beirut, so just do what I say. You won't regret it."

I asked him if I should be worried from the Syrian border guards. He calmed me down, but inside my head, I was scared that I might be taken directly from the border crossing to the military service without Noah knowing anything. I pulled myself together as I always did, and wore my best smile when we arrived on the Syrian side of the border. Until now, I think about how fast and smoothly everything went there after all the fears about leaving Syria. We left the car, and the driver told me not to say anything except if he asked me to. I felt he knew someone there after all these years of his job. I stayed quiet the whole time in that big hall full of counters and people; we went to a booth, and after greeting the employee, he just asked for my passport and an exit fee. He stamped my passport, and that was it.

I wanted to call Noah immediately or text him about our latest victory, but I knew the hard part was yet to come. I would better hold my seat belt tight enough.

Seventeen.

The second the car entered the Lebanese side of the border, a part of me was left behind—the part that didn't want to give up because of what was going on in my homeland, the part that always wanted to keep fighting to be who I am; another part of me was abandoned, abandoned only by me—it was the part that carried all the bad memories, the struggles, and the broken armor I always had on. I always knew it wouldn't be easier the moment I was in Lebanon, but I decided to leave that armor behind, which smelled like smoke and fire. I thought I could somehow forge a new one if needed. I was dead wrong because my shaky fingers could not even stitch a hole in a cloth; Lebanon twisted my fingers. They hurt till now every time I remember my days in this country.

On the way to the Lebanese border control center, the taxi driver stopped in front of a store. He knew the owner and asked me to change my black T-shirt to a white shirt. The first checkpoint stopped the car to scan the trunk; the driver hopped out to open it for one of the officers. He left his car door open, which seemed odd; no one asked for IDs or registration. While the driver was chatting with an officer, another approached the car's open door and slid his hand inside the accessory pocket under the armrest. I was shocked to see him taking money and a few packs of cigarettes. The driver had stashed them there for him. It seemed to be a standard procedure on the Lebanese side of the border.

We kept driving to the main building. "I'll give you the thousand dollars now, and don't you dare to say anything about where they are from. Just act normal because I am doing you a favor by giving you this money to show them. Otherwise, they won't let you enter," the driver made it clear to me.

Of course, I stayed quiet. I couldn't think of anything other than crossing the border to be with Noah. I had to enter the building alone. Hundreds of people were standing in line, and the Lebanese officers were shouting at them. I had to go to a window to show the thousand dollars in cash. They took them from me and checked whether they were fake. After that, I had to stand in another line to enter a second office, where they ensured that my hotel reservation was also confirmed. When my turn came, I handed them the reservation I had printed on paper. They called the hotel in Beirut and asked for a reservation under my name. The hotel confirmed so I could proceed to the next room, where a high officer sat behind a desk. It was in his power to decide if I could enter the country.

Now it was in his hands whether I might have a chance to be with Noah or I might never meet him. My hands were shaking. I observed the officer's mean face. He checked all the papers, my passport and my Syrian ID, and scanned me with his eyes. If he said Yes, I would have a chance to achieve many of my dreams; if he said No, it would be the end of my story because I would have to go back to Syria, and my life and dreams would vanish in oblivion.

He looked at me from head to toe and said: "No. Go out of my face. It is just a No." Was I going to give up that easily because of this, because of this power-drunk officer? What about Noah? I turned back to him and said politely, "With all due respect, and I know you are just doing your job, but what about my hotel reservation? I can't cancel it anymore, and the money will be gone. I am a university student in my graduating year and have only one semester left; this is my student ID." "Whatever, I will allow you only eight days." I rushed to the counter to get the entry stamps on my passport. I remember holding my phone up in the air, trying to get a bit of signal on my Syrian line so that I could text Noah and my mom. Sadly, it didn't work out.

I returned to the driver, and after he took back his thousand dollars, he couldn't stop bragging. According to him, he was the only reason they had let me enter Lebanon. We continued driving toward Beirut, and that whole time, I was trying to call Mirvat, my sponsor, from the Lebanese driver's number to ask for a meeting point. The plan was that she would pick me up. But her cellphone number was off —she had disappeared. I wasn't surprised because we could feel something fishy about her from the start.

I called my brother, told him all about it, and asked him what I should do now. My brother reached his friend in Lebanon to pick me up at a specific place on the way to Beirut. The driver took his hundred dollars, wished me luck, and left me where I had to wait for my brother's friend Adam.

I waited for more than an hour, sitting under the burning sun on a highway. I had only fifteen dollars left, no water or food— other than a bag of my favorite *Al Fakher* cookies, which I brought for Noah, as I had promised him. I was exhausted after forty hours with no sleep. All I could do was look around and remember that I was in a foreign, rough country with nothing; I couldn't even make a phone call to anyone or anywhere. Suddenly, a silver SUV car stopped in front of me. It was Adam. After greeting each other, we drove to the hotel.

On the way, Adam, who worked for a loaded Syrian businessman in Beirut, taught me the first lesson: "You look too decent and polite to survive in a place like Lebanon. Only the strong can survive this place." I didn't think much of what he had just said at that time. We started discussing Mirvat, and he told me he had not trusted her from the beginning and had a feeling she would play us until the end after she got all the money.

We drove to the Coral Hotel in the heart of the Al Hamra neighborhood in downtown Beirut. After checking in, I ran to the room to connect my cell phone to the hotel's Wi-Fi to call my Noah. He answered me with a voice full of worries and relief at the same time, "Babe! Where are you now?" "I am in Beirut, at the hotel. God, we will be together, my love." I couldn't stop myself from crying out of happiness. It was a tremendous victory, one of our biggest steps to be together.

That same day, Noah transferred me some money via Western Union to feed myself and to buy a Lebanese cellphone number until he would be in Lebanon. I went to the Western Union office and got the money without a problem. I bought myself some food, a Lebanese number, went back to the room and took my clothes off to shower and rest. When my underwear slipped to the floor, I saw my mom's and Noah's phone numbers written on the waistband inside, which I had scribbled the night before out of fear that something might go wrong or I might lose my phone. At that moment, I cried like a child, unable to believe I had made it.

That night, Noah booked his flight to Beirut. We planned to extend my stay in Lebanon with another hotel reservation until Mirvat, the vanished sponsor, would appear again. Maybe she would help organize my stay papers in Lebanon until I leave with Noah. That was still our hope.

Three days before my eight-day stay permission expired, I grabbed all the documents I needed and took a cab to the office where Syrians could extend their stay and deal with their papers. I had no idea about anything in that city and didn't know where to go or how much to pay for that cab. I ended up with a driver who drove in circles around Beirut before taking me to the stadium, where the center dealing with Syrian citizens was located. I later realized that he had asked for ten times more money than he should have earned from driving me to that place.

More than four hundred people were waiting for their turn at the stadium. The authorities registered my name. I had to take pictures in a small booth. Inside that booth was a guy wearing a uniform and using a smartphone to take pictures of people and then print them on paper. I still have these pictures, and every time I look at them, I ask myself: How could a person who looks broken like that even walk on his feet?

After standing in line for more than seven hours, I entered the main office and asked to extend my stay in Lebanon with another eight-day reservation in a different hotel. The two officers eyeballed me from head to toe and said, "What's this crap? Where's the official stamp of the hotel, and where is the hotel owner's signature?" I answered, "Sorry, but why do I need all that? Give me some slack. Can you call the hotel and check whether my reservation is legit?" The female officer raised her voice and got in my face, "Get what we are asking you for! The hotel is aware of these rules." After waiting all this time, I had to run to the second hotel, the Vie Boutique Hotel in the Verdun neighborhood, where Noah and I had a new reservation for eight days.

When I asked the employee at the reception front desk for the stamp and the owner's signature, she acted clumsy. I said, "The authorities asked for all this on my reservation paper, so what should I do now?" "We can't do anything about it. We don't do that for anyone." "But the officers there told me this is the rule. I have an eight-day reservation here and need what they asked me for." She gawked at me and disappeared into her boss's office for a few minutes. When she came back, she checked my name to find our reservation, "Well, we refuse to give you any of that, so just try to find another hotel that will."

When I left, the despair bubbled up like acid. I couldn't get what the officers requested, so why return to the stadium? Instead, I went to the Coral Beirut hotel and called Noah to brief him about everything. After a lengthy discussion and counting the few options, we decided that I would stay in Lebanon without any stay permit until Mirvat showed up to fix what she had brought on me. From that day on, I started speaking only English wherever I went, and whenever I had to talk with strangers, I felt safer not letting anyone know by my accent that I am Syrian.

I remember the day I had to leave the Coral Beirut hotel, the last day of my permit. I called Adam and told him about how I had tried to extend my stay in Lebanon, and he responded, "You must understand that Lebanon is a place where everything works with money and bribes. You are in the wrong place to be a decent person—you have been here for less than a week and are already drowning. Don't be afraid of being here without stay papers; you are not the only one struggling with the system."

Noah's flight would arrive at Beirut airport that night, and I remember being so nervous and scared of everything. I was worried that the new hotel, the "1866", next to the American University, might act like the one before. I was terrified that I was crossing my stay in Lebanon; I was nervous about my first meeting in real, face-to-face with Noah. I worried he might not like me, or he might find my messed-up life too stressful.

My dad gave me the cellphone number of someone he knew from the village who lived in Beirut for almost forty years. "He is a good man. You will feel safer around him," my dad assured me. This man, Abu Fadi, earned his money as a cab driver. I asked him to pick me up from the Coral Beirut Hotel and drive me to the "1866" hotel.

While waiting outside. I remember hearing two kids around the age of eight speaking a Syrian accent, and without even thinking, I looked in the direction of their voices. I turned my head to see them both on the floor cleaning the wheels of an SUV car with a big UNHCR sign all over it.

Abu Fadi arrived on time, and we drove around the neighborhoods, drinking coffee from the street sellers until we reached the new hotel. Abu Fadi was a decent man at the beginning of his seventies with a distinctive politeness. I told him about everything that had happened with the stay papers a few days before and what Mirvat had done to us. Abu Fadi heard stories like mine weekly with people like Mirvat. "It is the new trend of squeezing money from Syrians."

When I entered the hotel, I pulled myself together and wore my confident face with a smile. I went to the front desk, and they were professional and polite. They asked me about Noah and when he might join me; they handed me the room keys. It happened as smooth as that. I called Noah right away to show him the room and the bed we would share in less than twelve hours after waiting more than a year to touch each other. From the balcony, I saw a high building, its façade riddled with bullet holes, abandoned since the civil war in Lebanon. Now, Syrian refugees lived there, with no doors or windows. Shreds of fabric and old curtains protected them and their families from the cold. I said to myself, "Thank God that he sent Noah into my life; otherwise, I would live just like those people to survive if I ever made it there." I couldn't get rest or do anything. I could only wait in that hotel room till Noah arrived in Beirut.

Fifteen minutes after Noah's flight left Zurich airport, my brother called me to tell me that our half-aunt had returned from Italy and was currently in Lebanon. My half-aunt has Lebanese and Italian citizenship and always seemed free-spirited and open-minded. I considered her an inspiring woman during the three times I met her. She had grown up with my mom's mother and had left for Italy during the civil war in Lebanon.

I felt better and safer when I heard she was in Beirut. I even decided to come out of the closet to her and let her meet my Noah. After hanging up with my brother, I got excited and called her immediately. There was no answer, not even a signal. I checked Facebook and realized she had blocked me there. I went to WhatsApp and was also blocked there. I remember calling my brother again, whose answer was, "I know, she just hung up with me, and she doesn't want to be in touch with you." My half-aunt believed I was a dishonor to everyone with my "lifestyle." For her, my life as a gay man was an abomination.

My first thought was: "Grab a chair and wait for me to care." But deep down, I felt confused, stressed, betrayed again by a family member, and stupidly blind that I even had included someone like her in my prayers once.

I had to focus on one thing only: this amazing guy flying from his home country to be with me because he cares about me and loves me for simply who I am. Noah's flight took around three and a half hours. It felt like an eternity after waiting for so long to be together. I remember checking his flight on a flight-tracking website. My friend Thomas from Chicago had sent me the link. He wanted to make sure, step by step, that Noah and I would finally be together. I was sitting on the balcony of my hotel room, smoking and looking up to the sky, waiting to see the airplane. Suddenly, I could see the lights of an aircraft passing over the

Beirut skyline. I was ready for two hours, and all that was left was a bit of perfume. I ran downstairs to the lobby to wait there for my Noah.

In the lobby, I realized the hotel had three different entrances. One led to a small street in the back, and the other two to a mall with shops, restaurants, and a cinema. An escalator went to the hotel lobby. I decided that the best way to wait for my Noah was to sit in the lobby where I could oversee all the entrances. I was waiting and waiting and checking my phone screen every few seconds.

I heard the rattle of luggage wheels from the direction of the escalator, and I sat straight up. I saw someone's hair; the more the escalator went up, the more it revealed this person. Now I could see his face, his features. My heart was racing. It was the first time I could see my Noah in real life. I ran outside the lobby. I saw him leaving the escalator. Determined, he walked toward the exit that led to the small street. During these couple of seconds, millions of thoughts came to my head. Did he see me and run away already? Was he too nervous to meet me? It was obvious where the hotel lobby was, but instead, he left the building again.

Eighteen.

I did not doubt how much I loved this guy, no matter how he might react. I followed him outside and shouted, "Miin maa! Miin maa!" These were the only words I knew in Swiss German. Noah had taught me them. They meant: "My man!". He turned around, and I ran to him. We hugged tightly without saying a word for a while. I looked at his face. "I thought you saw me, and you wanted to run away." I remember his adorable laugh saying, "No baby, no, you are *miin maa,* and you will always be *miin maa*. I was craving a cigarette to calm myself down."

We took the elevator to the room and couldn't stop kissing, ignoring the security cameras. We made love the first thing we entered that room, and we didn't care about the open door or shades. It was a stage for the whole neighborhood.

Noah could smoke the cigarette he was craving—with me on the balcony of our room while eating one of the cookies I had brought from Syria for him, as I had promised. We went to bed together feeling exhausted, and I remember his touches being like hugs, and every hug felt like home. I remember falling asleep after looking at him, sleeping deeply, and my eyes refusing to shut to keep watching him.

We knew deep inside that there was still a long road ahead. The next day, We searched online for rooms to rent; we had the idea to contact one of the most known LGBTQ organizations in the Middle East, and we found the number of their office in Beirut. Noah sent them a message, introducing himself as a Swiss journalist in Lebanon who is meeting his boyfriend. The guy who answered at the organization was welcoming at first. During the conversation, Noah asked him for suggestions on safe areas for gay men in Beirut that we should investigate or for some contacts who might know more. The guy replied, "Yes, sure. We can give you some good suggestions." He asked Noah, "Your boyfriend is not from here?" Noah answered, "No, he is Syrian, and we have been together for over a year." And that was it. The organization never reached out to Noah for anything. I felt their attitude changed the moment they realized I was Syrian. After this, Noah understood what many Syrians had to endure in Lebanon without me saying a word.

We were on the run to find a place for me to rent and stay in because Noah had to fly back to Switzerland in five days. On the second day, we found an Australian looking for a roommate; I contacted him immediately, and when he heard my English, he felt comfortable and told me we could check the apartment if we were free. Noah and I had to react fast, so we agreed right away. We left the hotel and stopped a cab. A girl was already sitting in one of the back seats. It would be a shared drive, which is common in Lebanon. The cab driver was a man in his late sixties, and the girl sitting in the back was around twenty-two years old and a student at the American University of Beirut. Somehow, I couldn't speak Arabic with the driver—I didn't feel comfortable speaking Arabic anywhere in Lebanon. The driver couldn't speak English, so the girl spoke French with Noah and translated what he said about the address. I sat in the front next to the driver and stayed quiet the whole time. The driver, who assumed we were French tourists, started making fun of us with the girl. "I hate French people. They are such nickel nursers. They ruined Lebanon even more than Syrians did."

The girl arrived at her address, and after she had left the car, we continued the drive. I remember seeing the same store signs repeatedly, so I opened my phone, checked my GPS navigation, and realized we were driving in circles instead of in the direction we had asked for. The driver noticed I was checking the map on my phone and got nervous. I tried to prove to him

on the map that he was following the wrong direction.
At that point, it was too late to speak Arabic with him.
He might go nuts if he knew I had understood
everything he said before about Syrians and French.
He started shouting in the car and cursing with
disgusting street language, making me angry and
scared at the same time. Finally, he reached the area
we wanted to go to. He stopped the car and demanded
50 dollars. I looked back at Noah and then back at him
and said in English, "No, this's too much!" He yelled
at me in Arabic like a nervous donkey, "You know
what? You pay me 100 dollars! I drove you all around
Beirut!" He just wanted to rob the "French tourists."

Suddenly, he pointed a small pocket knife at my neck.
I felt the cold blade of that knife on my skin. Noah was
terrified and didn't know how to react. He told me to
give the driver whatever he wanted. I could feel
Noah's fear and begged him, "Leave the car
immediately!" Noah opened the door. "Please, just
give him whatever he wants. Please." The driver could
smell our fear like an animal and pressed the blade

even harder against my neck. I remember thinking of calling the police, but I knew they might deport me back to Syria right before Noah's eyes. I opened my wallet and handed the hundred dollars over. The driver took off the knife from my neck, pushed me out of the car while cursing, and sped away. I glared at the car disappearing in the bustling traffic of Beirut and felt nothing but weak, helpless, and humiliated. But somehow, we had both to pull ourselves together. We smoked a cigarette to calm down and walked to the address around the corner.

We knocked on the door where the Australian lived and checked the apartment. When we told him how much we liked it, he immediately agreed to share it. He would contact his landlord to set everything up. The following day, he texted us, "I am sorry. I really like you guys, but the landlord doesn't want a Syrian to live there, and he told me I better find someone else."

That same day, we had to go to the German embassy of Syria, which had moved to Lebanon after the war started. I had to get the stamps on my sister's and niece's passports. My brother-in-law has been a surgeon in Germany for years, so he sent visas for my sister and their daughter to reunite with him in Hamburg. As a brother, I could deliver the passports to the embassy and get the stamps. I called Abu Fadi and asked him to drive us there. The German embassy for Syria was in Rabieh, a posh suburb north of Beirut. The embassy itself, however, was anything but posh. It consisted of shabby white containers with mirrored windows that served as counters. In an open area with benches, people were waiting in the heat. Lebanese soldiers were responsible for the security of the facility. Again and again, they scolded the Syrians, who were waiting for their turn. Fortunately, I already had an appointment to get the visas on the passports.

I had to approach one of the windows to get a number for my turn. One of the Lebanese soldiers raised his voice, "Get lost! Did I allow you to come to get your number? I did not, so go wait over there with the others." After fifteen minutes, the same soldier passed us and heard us speaking English. It was obvious that Noah was a foreigner. He came to us and asked politely if I had a number. I answered him, "You asked me to wait, and I am still waiting as you said." He walked with me to get the number at the counter. Maybe he thought I was a German citizen, so I might complain, and he would get in trouble. We waited for almost three hours for my turn to come. I remember sitting there with Noah and speaking English with him all the time, so everyone thought that neither of us spoke Arabic. I eavesdropped on people's conversations, translating them to Noah. Most Syrians in this waiting area were women with children. Next to us sat a woman wearing a Niqab. Only her eyes were visible. She was talking with her four kids and was pretty strict with them. She tried to teach them how to behave later in the interview at the embassy and drummed into her oldest to try crying during the interview and to remember exactly what she had taught him to say. She was even threatening him. If he couldn't make himself cry inside the embassy, she would rub some chili on his fingers so he could touch his eyes during the interview.

Other women were talking about all the new clothes they had bought for their kids for this particular day to make a decent impression at the interview for the asylum visa to Germany. I remember all these happy kids, happy about nothing but wearing those new clothes like it was Eid or Christmas.

Later, it was my turn. I was standing in front of one of the mirrored windows; I thought someone would open it and talk with me, but instead, there was a speaker above the window where the employee started blaring orders through it while I was looking at my reflection on that mirrored window. The invisible employee opened a small drawer under the window and told me to place the passports there. "You can come back at three thirty to get them with the visa on. Next!"

Abu Fadi suggested visiting Jeita Grotto in the meantime. Water canals connected the big karstic caves, which had been formed over millions of years. Noah and I took a small boat, letting visitors explore the Grotto. We did not say a word to each other while being mesmerized by every detail we were seeing. The structures of that place reminded me of my own life. All those stalagmites and stalactites around us looked so beautiful and rough, the shapes of every one of them created by nothing but soft, cold water. They were simply pieces of art—a different type of art. The one that took time, strength, and determination to shape masterpieces like these, and all that beauty was hidden under the ground. I asked myself, "Am I going to be the water, or will I be the rocks? Can I be both? Am I being shaped beautifully by all the difficulties in the past and present?" I remember looking down and stretching out my arm to touch the water with my fingertips. It was cold, quiet, and clear. Would I be able to be like this water? This water, which can flow so freely. I wondered if the coming time would be like inside that cave or if it would be the same but filled with so much screaming and loud noise.

A few hours later, we stood in line again to get the passports and visas to send them to Syria. We had told Abu Fadi all about what happened the night before with the cab driver, and Abu Fadi promised we could call him whenever we needed a drive.

The next day, we found another studio for rent online, and we called Abu Fadi to get us there. The studio was around the Mar Mikhael area. According to Abu Fadi it was a good neighborhood to live in. It was a three-floor building on a corner, and the whole street smelled like gas from the highway nearby. The building was owned by an old Armenian Lebanese couple who welcomed us politely. When the woman knew I was Syrian, she said, "We love Syrians. They are our brothers and sisters."

The studios on the second floor were furnished with broken, run-down sofas and tables. Next to the bed was a small closet and a kitchenette. Sparse light filtered through the small windows. It seemed more than enough to survive Lebanon. Noah immediately hated both studios after he smelled the mold all over the walls. For him, a "VIP prison."

The couple took us downstairs to their apartment to discuss the tenants' monthly rent and the rules. The landlady started chatting with Noah in French, asking him where he was from in Switzerland and how he knew me. We had already prepared a cover story for situations like this. Noah told her he was here in Beirut as a journalist, and I was his translator, who became a close friend. It was a simple, small lie, but it was a lie that saved us from a lot of troubles while being in Lebanon. People were nosy, and every time we were asked about our relationship, we had to come up with this story to keep people's noses out of our lives.

The old lady showed Noah pictures of her daughter, "N'est-elle pas belle? N'est-elle pas belle? Isn't she beautiful?" she asked. I had mixed feelings when I understood what the woman had just said. I was amused by what was happening here in this living room full of kitsch and statues of the Virgin Mary; but then, I also felt teased and jealous. I could not say, "He is taken because he is mine." Or: "Sorry! But thank God he plays for my team and not for your daughter's one."

I noticed in the corner of the living room a big screen connected with cameras, which surveilled the whole house from the stairwell to the studios. They even installed one above every balcony. I tried to hide my discomfort. None of us was even thinking about staying in that place any longer.

Abu Fadi suggested driving us to the Gemmayzeh area for drinks and dinner. Noah and I found a restaurant and a bar on Armenia Street. That rooftop bar was the place for our first drink together. We talked nonstop— it was the date we had waited for so long. We knew we must catch any possibility of having a good time together because we never could be sure what the coming days would bring. At the bar counter sat two young women who behaved like celebrities, dressed in designer clothes from head to toe. They were talking freely, thinking that none of us spoke Arabic. One told the other how she was craving another drink, and the other girl answered, "You are kidding me. We don't have enough money to take a cab home, and you want another drink!" The first girl chuckled, "Oh, I forgot that we only look rich while we are here to pick up rich men." Her friend agreed. "Exactly, you are Lebanese, and you know better. So go back to work if you want more booze."

We woke up early in the morning to continue our hunt for a place to rent. Noah had to fly back to Switzerland at midnight the next day. We tried desperately to contact people who posted ads online. So many of them made it clear that they were not interested in renting to a Syrian. We started to contact private dorms for students and one of them answered.

Noah, Abu Fadi, and I met a man called Michel. He arrived in a black Porsche and parked right next to us on the sidewalk in front of a print shop he owned. After greeting each other, we walked together to the studio building in the Ashrafiyeh neighborhood. On the way there, Michel started eating my brain: From where do Noah and I know each other? And what am I doing here in Lebanon? But the most important thing for him was the pay. He asked me about my income, clarifying that I should pay the rent on time. When we arrived at the building, Michel was trying his best to show us that he was the boss in the building by showing off and talking with an attitude to the janitor, who was Syrian and lived with his family on the ground floor of the building.

The dorms were on the ninth floor in a formerly very spacious apartment, a T-shaped corridor connected to ten separate studios. Right in front of the main door was the one Michel wanted to show us. In the studio stood a small, wobbly bed with an old brown mattress and a pillow but no sheets or covers. On a desk was a portable electric stove. The tiny bathroom had a window to nowhere. From the studio's balcony, the view opened onto the concrete jungle of Beirut.

We didn't have much time or other options, so Noah and I immediately agreed to rent the studio. It was enough for us till we would be together somewhere else, safer and better. Noah and I grew nervous that Michel might ask about my stay papers, but he only cared about money. He asked for seven hundred dollars as a monthly payment and another seven hundred as a deposit. Michel told us to get the keys the next day, and all would be settled. We left his shop feeling relieved, but something felt still unsettling.

We checked out of the hotel the next day and moved to the studio. The bathroom had no running water. It was impossible even to take a shower. Noah was about to fly back to Switzerland in a few hours, and I remember both of us sitting on the bed whispering. There was a gap between the room's door and the floor, which didn't give us the feeling that we could talk to each other at a normal volume—especially since the studio right next to us was rented out to two Lebanese girls and we could hear their conversations loud and clear.

During the last few hours before Noah flew back home. I reviewed that week we spent together and felt rock-solid certainty that I couldn't live without him. We were both exhausted and just looking at the time, wishing it would stop so we could stay longer together. Noah was tired enough to fall asleep sitting on that bed. I studied every detail of his face to close my eyes in bad times and see only Noah's features to feel better and safer. I remember saying to myself, "He is the one with whom I want to grow old."

When he woke up, I cried between his hands out of fear of staying by myself without him on my side. He tried calming me down and repeatedly told me he had to return to Switzerland to check how we could officially authorize our partnership and get a Swiss visa. Nothing helped me other than his promise that he would come back; just hearing him say this made me feel safe and gave me something to look forward to. At that moment, I had to kiss his forehead, and that meant: "I can't live without you."

When Abu Fadi came to pick Noah up and drive him to the airport, I found myself in the same place where I had said goodbye to my mom the week before, the last time in Syria. I stood in the middle of the street bidding farewell to someone I love and watching the car drive away. When the car disappeared at the end of the street, I looked around and realized I was not home anymore. I was all alone by myself again. I heard my mom's voice inside of my head with the question she had asked me before I left Syria: "You want to live as a stranger your whole life?" I looked down at the dirty, cracked tarmac of this dark Beirut street and cried. I gazed up at the clear night sky—praying for everything to go fine. I didn't ask how, when, or even where; I just wanted everything to be okay and said, "I should not let a thing change who I am, but maybe the world should change its heart."

I couldn't close my eyes that night until I knew Noah had arrived safely in Switzerland. I stayed up until the morning, cleaning the room and fighting against cockroaches in that studio. After talking with Noah on the phone, I could go to bed and close my eyes, trying to sleep. I had no sheets or covers at all, so I covered myself with my clothes to keep warm until my mom sent me all my other clothes, some sheets, and a blanket.

I didn't leave that room for almost a week out of depression. And I was scared to get in trouble. Later, I left the house only to buy food from a nearby store. After the first week, Noah wired me the deposit via Western Union. I called Abu Fadi to drive me there so I could hand it over to Michel.

I remember standing in the Western Union office for thirty minutes while the employee was making phone calls and checking things on the screen before him without saying a word to me. I got slightly worried, but I tried to stay calm and remind myself that I had received money from Noah via Western Union before, so everything should be fine. The employee returned my passport and told me I should contact the sender because my name was blocked. I didn't understand why someone like me would be blocked. I called Noah. He was worried that Michel might kick me out of the room if we didn't pay him the deposit. Weeks after, we learned I had been blocked for simply being Syrian.

We had to find a way to pay Michel. He only accepted cash. Noah's friend and colleague at the newspaper agreed to transfer money to Abu Fadi instead. On the way to the Western Union office, I ran into Michel. He approached me and whispered in a threatening tone, "You know the rules. If you don't pay the deposit in less than a week, you better get out of here quietly, or I will help you do that with a big scene." I answered him politely, "No worries, I am on my way to get the money now." I returned to Michel's shop and paid him the deposit. I asked him for a receipt, and he said, "Yes, sure. I will come in an hour to the dorms to kick out some trashy girls and bring the receipt with me." I could feel something odd around Michel but couldn't really grasp it. I was the weak here in Lebanon, and he was in charge. In the afternoon, Michel showed up at the dorms with his kid, who spoke only French with him. He knocked on my door and started chatting with me about random things such as the Wi-Fi, which barely worked, or the "trashy girls," who were always partying. "If I were you, I would close the door," he said. He walked down the hallway, knocked on a door, and started screaming at the girls staying there. Michel, in his rage, called them all sorts of names, "whores" and "pimps," and threw their stuff out of the room and then out of the whole dorms to the stairs. I could feel that he was acting busy to avoid giving me any receipt. He knew I was scared and alone in Lebanon and took advantage of that. He also knew I was too polite and would never cause trouble. He used that against me.

In the coming days, I called Michel to tell him that Noah was visiting. He asked me, "Where will he sleep? You won't share the small bed, right?" I became so worried that I asked him for a mattress where I would sleep during Noah's visit.

Nineteen.

The day my Noah came back to Beirut, it felt like my blood rushed again through my veins. Noah was my spring after a heavy, cold, gray winter. When Abu Fadi drove to the airport to pick him up, I used to go downstairs to the street and sit on the sidewalk for hours. When Noah arrived, I couldn't even kiss him on the lips in front of Abu Fadi. We always had to wait till we were in the studio with the door and the curtains closed. That we had to hide our love was also a source of excitement and tension, fueled with high adrenaline. But every time I looked into this man's eyes, I just wanted nothing but to scream that I love him and let the whole universe hear it.

Noah called the Swiss embassy in Beirut and made an appointment to clarify our questions. The embassy was located in a high-rise building in the city center, near Martyrs Square. The entrance was guarded by armed Lebanese security and a dour woman in her fifties. She asked us harshly to show our passports. The second she became aware of Noah's red Swiss passport, she turned to an angel.

I felt like I landed on another planet when we entered the Swiss embassy. The elevator, which took us to the top floor, was like a trip from hell to heaven. Outside, the chaos of Beirut was buzzing with its stench of smoke and gasoline, with the trash piling up on every corner of the city. Now, I found myself in an organized and clean space with pictures of the Swiss Alps on the walls. Next to them hung a pair of skis as decoration and a poster of an art exhibition in Switzerland. The people working at the counters also seemed to come from another planet. They were polite, always with a smile on their relaxed faces. I immediately felt safe and welcomed.

An embassy employee came to the counter to ask how she could help. Noah gave her a short account of our story and asked about the documents we needed to register our partnership officially. The employee, who was so friendly, professional, and understanding, printed a list for us with all the documents required for the process. They requested around ten documents from Syria and a few others from Noah. Before I left Syria, I had already prepared many of them, translated them into German, and officially approved them by the Foreign Ministry. For the rest of the documents needed, I had to call my parents and ask them to send me all the approved and translated papers.

My parents managed to send them to me with a cab driver in the coming days. We had to meet him in a Beirut suburb after midnight because Syrian cabs were prohibited from entering the city center. Noah and I stood in the middle of nowhere till that driver showed up and handed us the documents out of his window:

my clean criminal record, for example, or the family and birth certificates. I had everything ready that day except for one paper I needed from Lebanon. It was the document that should officially prove my address in Beirut.

We went to Michel's shop to ask him for this paper. Michel told us to visit the *Mkhtar*. He would approve it for us. A *Mkhtar* is a position for a man who is usually old, known in the neighborhood, and knows everyone living there. Abu Fadi took us to the Makhtar's office. He knew how to deal with people in Lebanon better. After asking around, we stood in front of a run-down building and walked upstairs to the second floor, where the office was. We found ourselves inside a big bedroom with a big desk covered with dusty files—towers of files and papers seemed to grow like mold.

Behind the desk sat a guy in his twenties. "How can I help you?" he asked boldly. We were staggered by his young age. We told him we needed that document that approves my address, and he flipped at us right away and said, "You think you can simply show up like this here and ask for this paper? Where is your landlord? And why is he not with you?" Abu Fadi explained to him that the landlord was the one who had sent us here to get it and told him Michel's full name.

This young guy had already been rude to me when he knew I was the Syrian who wanted that paper. Then he looked at Noah disrespectfully and said, "What about you? You are the same, right? You better all leave this office. Don't come back without the landlord." I was so bemused at that moment. I can swallow everything except disrespect toward the people I love. But at that exact moment, Abu Fadi looked at the guy admonishingly, "Watch out and talk with respect; he is Swiss."

He apologized to Noah and stuttered in broken English, "Sorry, man, you not Syrian. Sorry, and welcome to Lebanon." A part of me felt satisfied that he apologized to Noah, but at the same time, I felt terrible and sad because me being Syrian made him dare to talk and behave with me like this. They say, "You can't force people to respect you, but you can at least refuse to be disrespected." I couldn't even do that. Again, I was the weak one who had no people or citizenship to protect him.

We started searching the neighborhood for another Mkhtar, and we were able to find one. He was an old, respectful man sitting behind a clean desk. Abu Fadi told him everything that had happened before, so the old man looked at me and said, "Sorry, my son, but there are people like this young guy everywhere. Just get any paper from your landlord with his ID information and signature. Ask him to write a confirmation that you are his tenant."

We returned to Michel's shop and told him about the whole hassle. He confirmed our suspicion that this young guy was actually not a real Mkhtar but the son of one. "He does this to get money behind his dad's back," Michel told us. Later, Abu Fadi learned through some friends that Michel had called the young guy to warn him that a Syrian guy would show up to ask for this paper, so he would better refuse to give it to him and get rid of all of them. But even without this knowledge, it was obvious that Michel resumed his power games with me to squeeze more money from us to get that piece of paper. He wanted me to beg him and humiliate myself for it. I had to give him what he wanted on a silver plate. I remember having a breakdown in front of him, begging him with my face wet with tears to provide me with the paper. After getting what Michel wanted and showing the Swiss guy how generous a Lebanese could be, he wrote all the information the old, respectful man had requested on a crumpled piece of paper. We returned to the Mkhtar and finished it in less than two minutes. All that was left to do was to translate the document into German or French and approve it in the Foreign Ministry of Lebanon.

That day ended way better than it began. Abu Fadi took us to the southern suburb of Beirut, where we ate grilled meat in a local eatery. Being in that area was a shock for Noah. It resembled nothing of what visitors from the west know of Beirut. This was a neighborhood of simple people trying everything to survive, doing their rough jobs on that main road, where a car mechanic could be right next to a grocery shop, which sold fruits and vegetables on the sidewalk above wooden timeworn tables. It was not the place for party people who spent their nights and money in Gemmayzeh and similar neighborhoods.

During Noah's stay in Lebanon, Michel knocked on our door at least once daily. We had the feeling he was trying to confirm his suspicions about us being a gay couple because he had never knocked on my door before Noah was there except once. He was always trying to sneak inside the studio for something that might help him prove whatever went through his mind.

I had to sleep on the Mattress most nights out of fear that he might try to enter the studio with the extra key he had. We felt we should prove him wrong with "normal" behavior until he dropped the habit of knocking on our door. We tried to be out of the studio as much as we could.

Noah learned about the opening of an exhibition at "Beit Beirut," a museum and urban cultural center, around the corner. That place offered a mixture of war remnants and modernity. Before the Lebanese Civil War, the apartment building had a photo shop on the ground floor. The exhibition showed all the pictures of the people who never picked up their portraits from the shop because of the outbreak of the war. The walls and ceilings of "Beit Beirut" were riddled with bullet holes. They served as a memorial for the civil war, which had ravaged the city. Snipers targeted anyone who approached the lines of demarcation through the bigger holes which faced the main street. Some words and sentences were scribbled in Arabic on the wall inside the sniper's room. They told the readers about love and poetry. They showed that even a cold-blooded person who kills quietly, hidden, and professionally could love, remember poetry sentences, or even draw a heart.

The exhibition was full of visitors from the upper class of Beirut who identified as the city's intellectuals. When we reached the third floor, we discovered another exhibition, which displayed photographs of the war in Syria. Seeing one picture after another filled my heart with nothing but pain. I tried to stop myself from crying and looked around me. All I could see was people behaving like celebrities with their glasses of champagne in their hands, walking around and checking every picture, acting like they felt it all and knew it all.

Noah's stay in Beirut was about to end again, and we felt the need to go out the last night. We checked bars and restaurants close to the studio. In Beirut, checkpoints were posted randomly everywhere, and we always feared they might stop us and ask for our IDs. The idea of a checkpoint asking for my ID and realizing that I had crossed the time of my stay used to terrify me. The image of being arrested right in front of Noah's eyes used to haunt me in my nightmares. It was the worst scenario that could happen for us. I knew Noah wouldn't be able to protect the one he loves. I remember overthinking this so many times a day. I knew that if I might be deported back to Syria, I could be drafted into the military service the second I crossed the Syrian borders. It would be impossible to contact Noah even if I still had his number on my underwear, as I could be stripped not only of my phone but also of my rights, my future, and even my soul.

We eventually found the Santana Bar in a street close by. We drank there together for hours and talked about everything in life, forgetting all the problems in front of us we still had to solve. They played a song in that bar, which my mom loved, and I broke into tears—I longed for her so much. Some people say "Crying unburdens the mind." For me, crying during that time was a simple, clear proof of how fragile I was. The tears in my eyes did the job of glasses. They showed me what I avoided seeing in myself every time I looked in the mirror. Somehow, it made me disrespect myself for lying to myself in my face in front of the mirror that I am strong and can handle everything. One of the uncountable reasons I fell in love with Noah is his ability to remind me of everything I survived on my own and what I can achieve without letting any pity be involved.

Noah had to fly back to Switzerland for his work and prepare his documents, which had to be included in our visa application file for the Swiss authorities. I never got used to the idea that Noah was leaving one more time to return after a few weeks. It always felt like the first time, or maybe even worse. I was sick of goodbyes to the point where it felt like I had an allergy to them.

The following day, I began the search for an official translator who would translate the confirmation of my address for the Swiss embassy. Michel told me he knew a French translator who would do it for me for a certain amount of money. He took triple the price I would have paid if I had done it through someone else. The next step was the official approval of my address document from the Foreign Ministry of Lebanon. I called Abu Fadi the same day I got the translated document, and he drove me there.

They asked for my passport, and the second they realized I was a Syrian citizen, they started scanning me from head to toe and investigating why I needed this paper to be approved. I told them about what the Swiss embassy had requested from me. They didn't believe me. "No embassy would ever ask for a document from a Syrian approving his address here in Lebanon." I couldn't argue with them because they simply needed an excuse for not doing their job. Abu Fadi took one of the employees aside and handed him some money as a bribe. He told Abu Fadi, "I need double of that. It is not easy to approve a paper like this for a Syrian. You know how the situation is." Abu Fadi doubled the amount, and suddenly, the employee's face brightened while talking with me. "No worries, we will make it work out. Just come back after a week to take it." Every day of that week felt like a year. I wanted nothing but to be able to take all the documents to the Swiss embassy and be done with it all.

After one week, I returned to that office in the Foreign Ministry; I realized that none of the employees Abu Fadi had bribed were there. I stood in line, nervous and tense. When it was my turn, I gave them my name and asked for my paper. They let me wait until one of the women who worked that day told me she couldn't find it anywhere. It was not even in the office's documented files. I called Noah immediately to tell him they had lost the paper or had just gotten rid of it. We had no other option but to start from zero again. I had to pull myself together and start everything again, paying the same money again and going through all the drama one more time.

I started to notice how my body was physically collapsing. I had an overwhelming feeling of suffocation, and the inability to breathe became my daily companion. I remember the moment I measured my weight and how shocked I was to see only 37 kilograms on the scale display. I remember the unbearable pain in my teeth; all I craved was a little rest, to sleep away from reality. I started falling asleep for the first time in my life with my eyes not fully closed—my brain was always working and fully ready if something would go wrong. Overthinking became my new addiction, and life permitted no time for a short rehab.

During this time, I felt exhausted not only physically but also mentally. Even my path itself was exhausted from my steps. I started to forget where home was or even if it had ever existed. I lost every memory of people who had visited my life or passed by; I had no clue what lay before me or on which shore I might be landing if I even would ever set foot on one. For some moments, I wished I was still a child who never grew older and stayed in the childhood port where the waves of life didn't sweep him away. Maybe these high waves came early to get me, and perhaps I just forgot time—while thinking I am the child, and the world is beautiful and safe. The truth is that the realm will always remain, and we are just damn visitors. I had to pull myself together after every breakdown repeatedly. With time, I became an expert in doing it faster and faster.

Long story short, approving the document of the address in Lebanon never happened; for many weeks, I repeated all the previous procedures. I had to do it over and over another three times, and the only answer I got was: "We can't find it. It just disappeared." I always asked myself this question about Lebanon: "If they truly want to get rid of Syrians, why do they make it hard or almost impossible?" For me, the answer was evident. Many Lebanese employers would lose hard and cheap workers. Landlords couldn't rent crumbling or abandoned apartments without windows or doors for exorbitant rental fees. Without the Syrians in

Lebanon, some Lebanese politicians would have no excuses for the issues of that failed state, plus the UN wouldn't pay millions of dollars for their expensive lifestyles anymore.

My brother heard about my struggle to get the address approved and reached out to Adam to check some of his contacts for help. Adam called me to say it would be easy for him to get approval; after all, he knew some bigwigs in the authorities.

A week before Christmas, my Noah came back to Beirut. It was the first time I could drive with Abu Fadi to the airport to pick him up. Abu Fadi assured me there would be no checkpoints on the way. At the airport, I was waiting for Noah in a corner, hiding behind a group of people. Noah had no clue; I came to pick him up. I remember seeing him from far away and sneaking between people until I stood behind him. All I wanted at that moment was to hug him or cover his eyes. But all that was impossible in a public place like Beirut airport. I started poking him discreetly. He turned back at me in surprise. Seeing his face in front of me and touching his coat made me feel alive again—believe me when I say: "Noah is my elixir of life." We drove to the Al Hamra neighborhood to eat Shawarma and returned to the studio. The streetlights were off, and we walked together in the deep darkness.

The next day, Adam called me to deliver the bad news. While trying to approve the paper for me, his contacts had to go through the fact that I had crossed my stay, thanks to Mirvat. She had taken a lot of money to sponsor me, and the second I entered Lebanon, she had disappeared. The authorities had become aware of my expired stay permit. "They might have to investigate you in person at a police station somewhere. They know your phone number and where to find you," Adam told me.

My knees gave away. I couldn't stand anymore. In one moment, I felt abdominal pain, vertigo, rapid pulse, and excessive sweating all at once. I was barely able to tell Noah what was going on. I remember him hugging me, trying to calm me down, asking me to breathe. He assured me there was a solution for everything. But this time, I couldn't believe it and felt it was time to give up on fighting the unknown. My main fear of being dragged away right in front of Noah's eyes or taken away after Noah went back to Switzerland boiled up again. He wouldn't know anything about me anymore.

Less than two minutes later, someone repeatedly hammered on the studio door. I remember looking into Noah's eyes. Pure fear was reflected in his gaze. I stood up and took a deep breath. My brain stopped functioning. I felt nothing at that moment anymore. But then I realized the time had come to protect Noah and me. Nothing should make me forget who I really was.

Behind the door, I could hear two men arguing about why I was not opening. I put my hand on the handle, my eyes closed. When I opened the door, my eyes opened with it. In front of me stood Michel, and behind him, in the dark hallway, was a man wearing some kind of uniform. Michel was talking to me. For a few seconds, his voice reached my ear distorted as if caught in the static of an old radio. When I could hear him clearly, it turned out that Michel had come investigating a complaint from an old woman who lived on the floor below. She was accusing the dorm tenants of throwing bleach above her laundry. The man behind Michel turned out to be the janitor. After listening to all their drama, I showed them my small inhaler, telling them about my breathing problems. "There is no way on earth I could have used bleach," I said. Michel insisted on checking around the studio to prove to the janitor the old woman was delusional.

My brain and body lost any connection to reality and everything surrounding me. I couldn't breathe anymore. My lungs felt like they were drowning in my tears. At the same time, the idea of even making a tiny noise was forbidden. Michel and that janitor were still standing and talking in front of the door.

Noah tried again to calm me down, to let me breathe. He held my face between his hands and repeatedly said with a trembling voice, "Look at me, just look at me. Everything is going to be fine." For the first time, I saw tears in my Noah's eyes. He always seemed strong and controlled and never let his emotions drive him during difficulties. But when I saw those watery eyes, I had no hesitation in mobilizing all the strength I could find to return to myself to protect Noah from my intractable life. I was like a ship in the middle of an ocean about to sink in the face of a violent hurricane. I had to use many buckets to get rid of the bad thoughts and the sorrows that were drowning me from within.

We decided to leave the studio—even if we would spend our time roaming through the streets of Beirut. The next day, Noah decided to go to the Swiss embassy early in the morning and tell them what was happening with the address paper. Our primary concern was the rest of my documents, ready and approved from Syria. They had an expiry date, which meant I could lose the chance to use any of them in the next few weeks. When we arrived at the embassy, we were welcomed by the same rude Lebanese woman and the armed security man we had encountered the first time.The woman's insolent behavior had not changed. She could tell from how I said *"Marhaba"* – "Hello" - that I am Syrian. The second she noticed Noah's red passport, she became a bit worried that Noah might complain about her rudeness after they had let us enter, so the security made sure every five minutes if someone had talked with Noah already.

When our turn came, the same employee who had helped us the first time called us to the counter. I remember how anxiety was feeding on me emotionally and physically—like a million leeches sucking my blood. Noah started talking in German with the friendly employee and told her briefly what was going on with the address document and his worries about the expiration date of my Syrian documents. She asked me to come to the counter to talk with her and asked in perfect Arabic, "Tell me, what's going on?" In my head, I tried to put our confused situation into words—

I was exhausted and tried to hold back my tears. Her simple question reminded me even more of everything we went through. I remember telling her, "I don't know what to say: every time I do the document, translate it, and try to approve it, they will tell me to come back in a week, and then the paper goes missing. I am worried about the expiration date of my Syrian documents."

The employee raised her hand and said, "It is ok; there's no need to continue. Do you have the document with the translation with you now?" "No, it is lost again." "Bring me the paper with the translation and come back Wednesday with all the other requested documents." Noah asked, "What about the approval?" "Everything you have is translated and approved except this address paper. I will send them to Switzerland, and they will decide there." Noah and I looked at each other, full of relief. We asked about the visa fee. "Let me check," the employee answered, "Because we never had to deal with a partnership registration between two men here before." She came back and wrote everything for us on paper, wished us all the luck, and said, "See you on Wednesday."

The night Noah had to fly back to Zurich, I didn't hesitate one second to go with him to the airport to say goodbyes—a part of me felt like I might not see him in a while or ever again. We smoked together outside the departure hall, and my only wish was that our cigarettes would never end. But, of course, the reality was merciless. We had to say goodbye. I couldn't show weakness, as it might be the last thing he could see of me, and it would make him more worried. I remember hugging him tight and letting him go through check-in while waving to him till I couldn't see him anymore behind the barrier. Our cigarettes had burned, but my heart became like a star with flames that never extinguished. Painful, eternal flames. Driving back to the studio without him was getting harder and harder out of fear that I might be taken away without even being able to let my Noah know. I used to imagine him all around the place, and I loved smelling him on the pillows, which always helped me feel safer.

I had to start over with the address paper and translate it for my appointment in the Swiss embassy on Wednesday. I remember being nervous that anything might go wrong at the last second, as it happened many times before. I could barely sleep the night before the embassy appointment. I stood on the balcony, looking up at the small piece of night sky I could see from there and praying for whoever was upstairs to protect me and help me through everything.

In the morning, I had to take a freezing cold shower because the power was off in the whole neighborhood. I got ready, talked with my Noah, and walked to the embassy downtown. When I arrived, my already famous rude Lebanese woman at the entrance asked, "You were here a few days ago, so what are you doing here again?" I answered her politely that I had an appointment today— and they let me pass. The friendly employee was standing behind the counter. When she noticed me, she smiled. She got all my papers and documents, checked them, and asked me to wait a few minutes. Those few minutes felt agonizing because my brain got used to the idea that I was somehow cursed, no matter how determined I played by the rules. The employee said, "Everything is perfect, and now it is time for the payment." I handed her the money required for the visa and went to sit again, waiting for her to get me the receipt. After a couple of minutes, she returned, and I could see in her face that something was wrong. I approached the counter; my hands were shaking. What would the problem be this time? She told me how sorry she was for giving us the wrong amount for the visa and that I still needed another hundred dollars because they had never dealt with something like our case in the Swiss embassy in Beirut. She looked helplessly at the papers and said, "Look, we close in an hour, but we work here till the afternoon today. I wanted to send your whole file to Switzerland before tomorrow's Christmas holidays. If you can get the money by the end of the afternoon, tell the security downstairs that I told you to come back. He will call me and let you in."

I left the embassy thinking of ways to solve the problem as fast as possible. I knew only one thing for sure: I couldn't let the whole thing be delayed till New Year. I called Noah immediately to brief him, and he said, "Okay, baby, don't freak out. I will wire the money to Abu Fadi." Abu Fadi agreed to bring me the money right away, but I had to come back to the area of the studio. I remember running like a sprinter. I arrived at my studio's location, but Abu Fadi was not there; I waited and waited for him, thinking he might be stuck in traffic. At some point, I called him as I was running out of time. Abu Fadi answered. His car had broken down in the middle of the road. I ran a few kilometers to reach the corner where he was. Thick smoke billowed out of the hood of his cab. I had to rush back to the embassy before the end of the working hours.

In front of the building, I gasped for air like a drowning man, but with a big smile on my face. When the employee saw me, I could feel how happy she was and how much she wished Noah and I would be together soon. She took the payment, gave me the receipt, and stamped the official confirmation of my application for the Swiss Visa on my passport. She told me she would send the papers to Switzerland as soon as possible.

Noah and I needed a victory like that to push us forward, and we knew that our trust in the Swiss authorities was rock solid. We deserved to be together; they would help us based on logical paragraphs. I remember walking from the embassy to where Abu Fadi's car had broken down. It was a walk that I hadn't taken for many years. It was the walk where I carried hope and felt my heart beating again. I could see the world's colors again—even if every inch of my body and every space of my mind felt pain.

I walked back to Abu Fadi and thought nothing could ruin my day after this great victory. Abu Fadi sat in the car and waited for the towing service. I threw myself into the passenger seat and told him about the Swiss embassy and how happy I was. Suddenly, I felt my phone vibrating. I was surprised to see an "Unknown Number" calling me. I answered. "Is that you?" a man asked me, saying my full name. I got nervous and answered him, "Yes, who's asking?" The man ignored my question and said, "Where are you now? I can hear the traffic, so you are not at your place." My voice turned shaky. "Sorry, but who's talking? Who are you exactly?" The stranger began to laugh scornfully. "Who am I? Are you sure you want to know? I am from the General Security Department in Beirut. This is who I am."

Twenty.

I remember how I started shaking in the passenger seat of Abu Fadi's car and how he looked at me with a worried expression. "Are you okay, son? Why did your face turn pale?" I went silent for a couple of minutes while the man on the phone repeatedly asked insistently, "Where did you go? Did you become mute suddenly?"

Eventually, I could pull myself together and keep talking with him. He wanted to know my date of birth and if I was working while in Lebanon. He asked me again, "What are you doing outside? I can hear the traffic." I told him I had just come from the Swiss embassy, where I had applied for a visa. Of course, he didn't believe me and thought I was making it up after knowing he was from the General Security department. He continued his inquiry. "What are you doing during the days and nights?" "I am always home and go out only to buy food every few days." And, of course, he didn't believe me again. I could hear the rustling of paper. Apparently, he took notes of everything I was saying. At the end of the call, he said, "We might call you again to make you come to the police station for a few questions."

I left Abu Fadi's car and ran to a sidestreet between the buildings to call my Noah. The second I heard his voice, I burst into tears. I was terrified to return to the studio and even to go to the neighborhood and walk through its streets. The Lebanese could catch me everywhere. I talked with Noah for more than an hour while crying nonstop. I had no clue what to do or where to go, and not having enough sleep for a long time made me overthink and see only the bad scenarios that could happen.

Somehow, I had to pretend to Noah that I felt better after talking with him, but that was not the whole truth. I just wanted him not to worry about me. I knew he couldn't do more than he was already doing. There's nothing more agonizing than to see the people you love in real danger while you are helpless. I decided to walk slowly to the studio. It took me more than four hours till I dared to enter the neighborhood. When people hear something like this, they might say I was overreacting, but the reality is that I had been in a situation like this before, when I was asked to come to a police station for a few questions and then vanished for days. All of that had happened in my own home country, between my people, under the sight of my own family, and no one could save me from that terrible trauma. You don't need to be a psychotherapist to make a diagnosis. I was deeply traumatized and stressed from a young age.

When I reached the studio's building, I climbed the stairs slowly, trying to grasp every little noise from the top floor. What if the security police were waiting for me behind the dorm's door or inside the studio? From that day on, I lived in complete darkness, with no lights on, avoiding to make any noise. I was so terrified that I prepared a text message on my phone: "Noah, baby, I love you even far beyond what people say love is. They just took me away. I am sorry! I couldn't have a better life, so you didn't have to go through that with me. Don't be sad and don't come to Lebanon, because there's nothing you can do. I will survive whatever comes next. You know me how expert in surviving I am—I was born to have all sorts of unfairness in life, but I promise you, I will survive it all because I am not allowed to lose any single fight, no matter what." I prepared this message to be sent to

Noah with one touch on my cellphone in case anything terrible happened.

I put myself to sleep thinking: "Why the fuck don't we learn to deal with things like this at school? Why did no one tell us how hard it is to face unfairness in life? Isn't that more important than math or religion, or battles that happened centuries ago because of the decisions of some fartheads? Don't we need our mental health to build our societies? Obviously, this is the last of anyone's interests."

Christmas came, and I had only myself inside that cold studio; I was far away from everything and everyone I knew and loved. I remember opening the curtains every fifteen minutes to catch a glimpse of Christmas trees inside the apartments in the buildings surrounding me, where families and friends had nothing to do but enjoy and celebrate their time. Christmas has always been important to me as a child. Which child doesn't love gifts? As I grew older, Christmas was the day we would have a big tree and eat delicious food my mom had prepared for hours. The smell of food wafting from the apartments made me crave my mom's cooking. When she had the opportunity, my mom sent fresh cooking with a driver to Beirut, especially when my Noah visited. Sometimes, the food arrived still warm. But that Christmas, I had nothing from my mom except the memories of her and my dad laughing and being happy. These memories nourished me.

I called my brother and Adam to explain the situation the next day. Adam assured me he would use his contacts to check what was happening; my brother also tried to reach out to everyone who might help. On a Sunday evening, I got a call from a strange number again. I hesitated to answer, but I had to. It was Mirvat. I didn't know how to respond when she said her name. She started crying on the phone and telling me that she never meant to harm me. Now, she wanted nothing but to help and meet me in the neighborhood. It turned out that she lived only a minute's walk away from the studio.

I was worried about meeting her. My brother told me
that Mirvat had heard through her contacts in the
General Security that I got this call, and they might ask
me to come for an interrogation. Now, she was
anxious I might bring her name up and tell them the
main reason why I was forced to cross my stay in
Lebanon. I might tell them all about the money she
took from us in exchange for sponsoring me to get a
one-year permit in Lebanon. She had to save face and
show me what a good person she was. That she never
meant to harm me.

Noah encouraged me to meet Mirvat despite
everything. We needed any help possible. I texted her
and told her where we could meet. I remember how
nervous I was leaving the house to meet one of the
people who got me to be in all the shit I was going
through. Mirvat arrived fifteen minutes late in her blue
car and parked on the sidewalk. She left the car to hug
and kiss me on the cheeks. Her voice sounded
hypocritical; the woman was aware of her guilt. At the

same time, she knew I was weak, and she was strong here, even though I had the right to tell the General Security all about her and about what she did to me.

I sat in her car, listening to all her lies about why she had vanished when I entered Lebanon. While she was crying nothing but crocodile tears, the side mirror of a passing car hit her car's mirror, and all of a sudden, the guilty, innocent Mirvat transformed into a bizarre, insolent, and ill-mannered person. She tore open the door in a fury and started screaming at the woman driving. "You whore, you fucking bitch, you need someone to fuck you in your ass? This is why you are in a hurry. Don't think I am a woman because I can take my dick out now and stick it in your mouth in front of the whole street." Shocked, I slid down the seat so no one could see me. The other woman ignored Mirvat's screaming. This only enraged her even more. Mirvat marched through the dense traffic to the other vehicle, hammering on the windows and scratching the paint with her keys. I was stunned to see anyone behaving like this. When she was done with her furious crusade and the other woman managed to escape, Mirvat returned and immediately changed to her usual tone. I had no idea why she behaved like this in front of me. Did she want to show me that I couldn't mess with her? Or she tried to show me that she was out of her mind? "Sorry, but she needed a lesson," she said. I ignored her and brought up our main topic again: the General Security. She was willing to help and would use all her contacts to find a solution.

On Monday noon, my phone rang. I knew right away that it was the General Security. I answered after taking a deep breath. The man on the phone started asking me the same questions they had during the first call. I responded politely, and when he finished his questionnaire, he said, "That's all correct." "You must appear at the police station at this address on Wednesday at nine in the morning for further questions. If you don't show up, we know how to get you here in ways you won't like."

When he hung up, the fear crawled back into me. But

at the same time, I felt calm. I knew I couldn't do anything about it, and neither could Noah, so what was the point of making him more worried about me? Adam promised he would do his best to contact everyone who could assist. My brother fought with Mirvat that day, blaming her for the whole situation. She reached out to me right away and said she had called a high officer in that police station to help. She would come with me. The thing was that Mirvat wanted to be present there to control the situation in her favor. She wanted to make sure I wouldn't bring her name up and put all the blame on her. In the coming days, I barely slept. Eventually, Adam told me that an officer known to him called the head of that police station. He would also promise help.

To make myself feel better, I scrolled up and down the conversations between Noah and me on my phone during the last two years. I knew I had no rights—no rights as a Syrian, no rights as a gay man. I knew they could easily check my cell phone or even take it from me, which also meant they could figure out I was gay.

Noah and I decided to delete everything on my phone showing we are a couple, every picture of Noah and me kissing or hugging, pictures of our first night together shirtless in bed, pictures that helped me feel safe and fall asleep for so many nights. I had to delete more than two years of conversations between me and my love and make every clue that we were together vanish.

I was so scared to call my Noah the morning of the subpoena. It might be the last time I could talk with him or even hear his voice. At night, I called him to make him less worried about me, and hearing his voice always made me feel better. I will never forget that phone call when Noah and I said goodbye to each other. We said everything that could be said and left to be said because we knew we were in a situation that easily could be the farewell. At the end of the call, we waited until the other hung up.

On the morning of the subpoena, I struggled with flashbacks from the time when I had to go with my dad to the police station in Syria for "questioning" and vanished for a few days; then and now, I was nothing but helpless. The first time, I was with my dad in my own country, but this time, I had no one I could trust or feel safe with, in a foreign country that despised my people, in a place where everything works only with money and influential contacts.

Before I left the studio. I took a long shower because I had no idea when I would have the chance to take another one. I was freaking out more and more, one second after the other, till my brain shut down. I stopped thinking about anything. Mirvat came to pick me up, and from the second I entered her car, she didn't stop talking. Her voice sounded like a cartoon character. When we arrived at the General Security, I was like a walking dead, a mass of flesh with no soul and no emotions left. Mirvat called this "officer" she knew, and he met us at the gate. The "officer" turned out to be just a security guard who started flirting with her in front of me. He shook my hand and said, "Let's hope we will fix everything." Mirvat told him about Adam and the officer who talked with the head of that police station. The guard looked at me and said, "Wow, you know our boss, this is a good start." I stayed quiet the whole time, trying to control my feelings as much as possible.

I remember entering the building and skipping a long line of people who wanted to get some documents. They stared at us, wondering why we crossed the line without passing the security check. We took the stairs a few floors up while Mirvat and that man were flirting as if they met in a nightclub. On the way, we came across a teenager who was around fourteen. His features showed no emotion at all. His hands were cuffed. On another floor, I saw a policeman slapping an old man who looked nothing but poor and helpless. We reached the department of the highest officer, the one Adam had talked with and had given my name. "The boss" was waiting for me.

When we entered his office, I said nothing but a stifled hello. The highest officer was an older man with a modest and serious appearance. He gazed at me and said, "Fine, just go to the investigators now." We left his office and walked toward the investigation room at the end of the hallway, where a security guy pushed another teenager roughly out of the door. Witnessing this made me use the last energy I had left to avoid a breakdown in the middle of that hallway.

The investigators asked us to take a seat and chatted with Mirvat for a couple of minutes about random things. It was obvious they were hitting on her while my heart was about to stop out of fear. At some point, one of the investigators asked me, "So, do you know why you are here?" I answered with a low voice, "Yes, I guess I do." "Why are you worried? You know our boss; we won't eat you." He started asking me the same questions they had asked me twice already on the phone. "So, why did you stay that long in Lebanon? We gave you only eight days. You are breaking the law here."

I remember looking at Mirvat, and all the emotions and feelings I had bottled up exploded in a part of a second. I couldn't lie, and at the same time, I couldn't tell the truth that Mirvat was behind all of that — next to my bad luck with everything before. I was always terrible at lying, so I developed some hiding abilities to survive in these societies. But in this investigation room in Beirut, I felt like hiding meant lying, and I couldn't do that. The more I thought about all of this, the more I cried, and the more I felt that I couldn't breathe anymore. My face turned red, so they gave me a glass of water to calm down. I took my inhalator to help me breathe.

I told them about everything that had happened without mentioning Mirvat's name or what she had done with me. I assured them that I had tried everything I could to extend my stay with the second hotel reservation but that it didn't work out because of how I was treated by the employees there and the owner's refusal to approve the reservation with the stamp and signature. The investigator shook his head. "But there isn't a law like this." I told them how much I struggled with the address document, how many times I had to redo it, and how it always went missing in the foreign ministry of Lebanon. I told them that I was not leaving the studio except to buy food and to be with my Swiss friend who's coming to visit sometimes. I also informed them about the Swiss embassy and the visa I was waiting for. They asked for proof, so I showed them my passport with the official stamp from the Swiss embassy. I remember how he looked at me and said, "It is okay. We heard enough." He looked out of the window for a whole minute. Everyone was on pins and needles, waiting for him to say something more than that. Then he looked back at me and declared, "We wish everyone we deal with would be at least one percent of what you are. You are so polite, decent, well-raised. Rare to find these days." I was speechless. I felt it was my right to hear something that showed me that people like me wouldn't always be thrown under the bus and be victims of the system or others' mistakes.

They told me that as long as I would stay out of trouble or avoid wrong places, no one would bother me, which I couldn't believe based on my personal experience in Lebanon. After leaving that office, Mirvat bragged about how her contacts had helped with the situation. When we walked to her car, she made a promise. "No one will drive you to the airport to leave this shitty country other than me. We made it." I couldn't respond to that other than with a fake smile.

I always used to call my Noah at a street corner, where garbage was piled up in large trash containers next to the dorms. No one used to walk by, so I could talk freely and clearly instead of whispering in my room. I left Mirvat at that spot and immediately called Noah with tears of relief and happiness. I told him I had been treated well, thanks to Adam's contacts. God knows where I would be otherwise. I remember telling Noah how scared I was. Still, deep inside, I always had this feeling that buried fear alive. It was the firm conviction that things would always be fixed in my life no matter what, as I always had these strong beliefs that didn't always match reality. Still, people with good intentions will always get back something good somehow—no matter how long or hard it might be. I returned to the studio and couldn't remember the last time I slept that deep.

New Year's Eve came. Years ago, at a very young age, I learned how to be alone and enjoy my own company. I decided to teach myself to deal with loneliness and learn how to be my own best friend without needing others. At that point in Beirut, I was already used to living in the dark, so I spent that evening just in that unlit room with the curtains open. The other apartments gave enough light to see my full ashtray.

Already as a teenager, I sometimes spent New Year's Eve alone in my room, wishing to be in a place where I could fit in. At that time, I couldn't appreciate enough the meaning of the voices of every family member in the living room enjoying their time. I didn't know that dreaming of being in a place where I could fit in would lead me to isolation. That longing overshadowed the real task: planning for the future.

Sitting in the dark studio with nothing but the glow of my cigarette, I remembered a conversation with Lara many years ago. I had considered Lara my best friend for most of my life, but not anymore. We discussed the war and the situation in Syria in front of her family and friends. I told her that one day, I would leave the country and live where I could be happy and accepted for who I was. Lara said, "What about you stop fooling yourself and filling our ears with shit and dreaming above the clouds? One day soon, you will be dragged to the military service, and you will be nothing but a poor soldier on the front lines, eating wet rotten bread and crying about how fucked up your life is."

That New Year's Eve, I remembered this conversation like I was living that moment all over again. I felt the same anger. I felt hurt that Lara, out of all people, had thrown these words in my face. I remember how I raised my finger and said, "Sorry to bring you bad news from the future, because I will prove you so damn wrong. Ten years from now, let's see where you will be, how you will be, and where I will be, and how I will be." Recollecting this answer made me feel strong all over again and recall who I truly am. I reflected again on my gift to always rise after falling, and my talent for making whoever kick me while lying on the ground pray that I would never rise again. I could feel that resoluteness was driving inside my veins instead of my blood. Something shouted once again that I would survive everything, and no life supernovas would break me. Instead, they should make me reborn as a better version of me from yesterday.

That midnight, I decided to pay no attention to the fireworks and ignore even hearing their fizz and swoosh, denying considering New Year's Eve as one, denying calling it one. For me, it was all about being with the people I love, so I refused to let it even exist that year—it was not what I wanted it to be, as simple as that. I called my parents to wish them a happy New Year without mentioning anything I had been through. Seeing their faces through my phone screen every day was the wall I always leaned on.

An hour later, it was midnight in Switzerland. Noah spent the night with his best friends from New York, Germany, and Denmark to celebrate. Saying hello to them and seeing them sitting around Noah's place made me wish nothing but to be there and have an ordinary New Year's Eve instead of my denied one. I talked with Noah afterward, and all I can remember was how much we were both trying to act like we were doing okay, spending that night away from each other, but believe me, we were both terrible actors. After that, I decided to go to sleep, and while brushing my teeth before bed, all I could think of was Noah and I standing every night next to each other to brush our teeth in front of the mirror. When I woke up the following day, I wished to open my eyes to see my Noah sitting beside me in that old small bed, reading his "New Yorker" and waiting for me to wake up. I opened my eyes to see no one and nothing but those molded walls. But I opened my eyes with a smile decorating my face. I looked around me and appreciated those molded walls for being my shelter till I was out of there—with no one other than the love of my life.

Twenty-One.

Growing up, I thought I successfully passed every test of loneliness on my own. I became a stronger version of myself. I believed I already graduated from that school with a high average. The ugly truth was that what I had already passed felt like a kindergarten level compared to what I had to endure in the coming months. Days passed by, and none of them were easy on me; loneliness was feeding on my soul, but I refused to give up, thanks to my previous education in this field. Noah couldn't come to Beirut anymore. He made sure to send whatever the Swiss authorities requested from us as soon as possible, which led him to stay there, always ready to deal with everything. Depression was always looming, but I was focused and smart enough to see the real meaning of it. It is a prison where we play the two primary personas, the imprisoned and the jailer himself.

I made myself busy with anything that came to my head. I started drawing and designing leather bags, but only on paper. I started walking every day for at least twenty minutes, but only on the two-meter-long balcony. Listening to music has always pulled me out of so many dark places throughout my life, but it wasn't even possible to listen to any music in that place. The Wi-Fi in the dorms worked maybe only a couple of hours once a week, and using my mobile data was not even an option. I had to save it to talk with Noah and my parents. I remember waiting and checking the Wi-Fi signal for the whole night, and the second I received one, I tried to listen to the songs I needed to hear. Every thought was a battle, every breath was a war, and I didn't think of winning until I listened to some music again.

If you grew up in any Arabic-speaking country or one of the Middle Eastern countries like mine, you would have the same image I had of Switzerland. Switzerland has always had this image of peace and neutrality, the only place with real democracy, the place that is heavenly beautiful with the Swiss Alps and the charming lakes. You would see a painting or a picture on a living room wall of an idyllic Swiss landscape. In the house I lived my whole life in, in Syria, hung a couple of them. If you grew up where I grew up, you probably heard the saying "*Mank bi Suisra Habibi*," - "Wake up, you are not in Switzerland, sweetheart." Whenever I mentioned something about longing for a better life or being treated better, I used to hear this from everyone: "Wake up, you are not in Switzerland." Growing up and hearing this saying all the time made me live with the fact that Switzerland was an impossible dream that I never even dared to dream of. In the past, I always read how exclusive and expensive Switzerland is, how strict it is for giving a visa, and how difficult it is to get one; that was something that made me admire it all the way, but still, I never dared to dream about even going there, I had to always dream about the possible, not the impossible to protect myself from disappointment.

At some point, the universe brought me to the position of going through the experience of achieving an impossible dream. Noah always made it clear to me how strict Switzerland is regarding immigration, but he also stressed how fair the system is. He had trust in his country and its system, so he passed this trust to me, too. We were always confident of who we were and what was between us, and we both believed we would go all the way to prove it to the whole world— if we had to. It is common to hear this last sentence, but have you ever considered proving it to some authority? To prove a relationship is never easy, and when you are in love, you will believe that you can do it, even by mentioning the smallest and simplest things you share with your partner, whether rings or matching t-shirts. The question is, how can we describe and prove love to an official authority—to be together and never be far away from each other ever again?

During the first few months of the new year, Noah was always on the run, preparing everything the authorities requested and sending all the documents. The Swiss authorities were doing their jobs, nothing less, nothing more. They sent Noah a list of questions he had to answer, one by one: how we got to know each other, where and how often we had met. Noah wrote them a letter in which he told our story from the start—without mentioning any of the struggles we have been through because he was convinced his country would have understanding enough for what a gay couple like us might be going through. When answering the question, "How do you keep in touch as a couple?" My Noah spontaneously came up with the idea of sending them a list of our phone calls over the last few years. There were also the questions "Who proposed the idea of being together first?" and "How do you see the future for both of you?" Many people might feel pressured by such questions; we looked at the Swiss authorities as an ally who could support us in being together. The Swiss authorities wanted nothing but to hear a real story; they wanted to listen to the truth.

The idea of being trapped somewhere always terrified me, even more so, as it wasn't in my hands whether I could leave. Beirut and Lebanon, in a bigger picture, were my prison. The thought of not being able to go back to Syria or not being able to be with my Noah tortured me every single day. I used to leave the studio once or twice a week to buy some food, and every time I did it, it was because of Noah begging me to go out and take a walk; he was always worried about me, and I was also worried about myself. During that time, I reached a weight of thirty-six kilograms. I remember avoiding looking in the mirror to maintain a strong image of myself. I always avoided calling my parents on video call so they wouldn't see how skinny I had become. I didn't want anyone, including myself, to witness seeing me vanish more and more. Except Noah — Noah was the only one on earth I knew he would love me no matter how I looked.

Noah had to fill out the same application for a registered partnership we did in Lebanon, but this time in Switzerland. He sent it to the immigration authorities the same day, a Thursday. Noah and I talked about everything daily, but in the last couple of weeks, we didn't dare to touch the topic of our reunion. During the weekend, depression hit me hard. I used almost a full inhalator in those two days. After talking with Noah on Sunday night, the tremor I experienced was terrifying. I remember how I fell on the floor, shaking uncontrollably like an epileptic. I experienced one of the worst feelings of loneliness in my whole life. I had no one around to do something about that attack or make it stop, and even *I* was helpless to make it stop. I experienced my body losing faith in me. Its tremble was like a revolution, a declaration of independence. My body spoke its own language, announcing nothing but breaking up with me. I remember my brain acting neutral, trying to calm things down to fix things between us—my body and me. I remember my brain pushing into my consciousness nothing but a few pictures Noah had sent me that morning—photos of the snow from his bedroom window in Zurich. I repeated to myself, "This is what you will see one morning soon when you wake up." The rational path my brain followed helped my body to readjust again, reconsidering that no one of us exists without the other—that we started something together and have no other option but to finish it together. The brain believes, and the body achieves. This is what I had experienced before; my body started collaborating, and I had the power to crawl up to the bed while nothing was rushing through my head other than those pictures of the snow, which later helped me fall asleep. But let's be honest: what dreams gather and collect, awakening disperses.

I always knew I was a sensitive and emotional human being—maybe too sensitive. When I was a kid, my mom told me, "You better try to control how sensitive you are; otherwise, you will suffer a lot in this world." With time, I could control it by hiding it. I was never able to kill it and never wanted to because I accepted a long time ago who and what I am. I could strip it out of its colors and make it transparent so that most people's senses couldn't even feel it in the room. I am also emotional, which many people consider a weakness. I have heard it many times from the people closest to me, but let me tell you something about emotions: They make us alive. Every time I cried, I felt somehow better— crying was my natural pain killer instead of reaching the help of drugs or alcohol. Being emotional made me always honest with myself and who I truly am. Being emotional always showed me to naturally separate right from wrong and helped me remember to focus on myself. Ultimately, we all need to become a good version of ourselves. The right and healthy number of emotions can build empathy toward ourselves. But at that time, emotions became some cancer. They were too overwhelming, and they were feeding on me. Time became an enemy because of my fear of it.

On Monday, my Noah begged me to go and take a walk, even if it was around the building. Noah and I opened the topic of being together soon, and my biggest fear was that he might give up on us. I always needed to hear him affirm that he loves me just like I love him—over and over again. I go back to our conversation on the phone and to something he said, "We finished everything with the papers, baby, we did all we had to do, and we did our very best. I sent the last paper on Thursday, and today is still only Monday, so we need to wait a bit more. The immigration authorities have so many cases other than us to deal with—we must prepare ourselves for everything. We will not stop fighting to be together, but it might take longer than we wish for."

Everything he had said was simply true, but I couldn't think anymore, couldn't worry nonstop; I needed to let go and shut my thoughts down. That bitter winter in Beirut crept into my feelings and froze them. After talking to Noah, I went to the room and filled the bathroom sink with water. I needed to scream so loud, and I had no other option than to scream underwater so no one could hear how much in pain I was, a pain that could drown the whole world. I went to bed immediately and fell asleep in less than a minute, trying nothing but to run away from that world and shut everything down.

Noah and I never called each other without texting first, and we both had this habit of writing "Can I call?" before actually calling each other. I opened my eyes to see Noah's name on my phone screen. He was calling me, and the first thing that crossed my mind was to check if he had texted me already. But I saw no message from him; the ice cap around my feelings melted right away, and I had a million thoughts about what could have happened and what new problem we would face now. I answered him and asked right away, "Babe! Is everything okay?" Noah repeatedly replied with a choked voice, "It arrived."

I had no idea what he was talking about, so I kept asking, "What has arrived, babe?" Then he said something that my ear picked up, but my brain didn't process. Noah kept repeating this one word, and at some point, my brain understood. "Visa." – "What do you mean?" "Baby, your Swiss visa has arrived, and we will be together soon. You must contact the embassy to get the visa stamped on your passport. I will come to Beirut and book the return flights for both of us the second you get the visa."

While listening to what he had just said, I burst into tears. I was happy to the point where I forgot to breathe. I was happy to the point where I left the bed and started jumping while crying and shouting, "God, we made it! We made it!" For the first time in my life, I was above the clouds and far beyond that. I remember how hyperactive I was that night; I felt I shouldn't sleep because I had to enjoy every second of this news. I wanted to feel happy as long as possible. The visa was not on my passport yet, and there was still so much to deal with, but I refused to let any worries ruin my happiness.

The next day, I called the Swiss embassy and spoke with the employee who had dealt with our file. I told her that Noah got a letter from immigration stating that the visa had arrived, and I should contact the embassy as soon as possible. She was so glad for us and asked me to come the next day to leave my passport at the embassy.

The following morning, I returned to the embassy, where they took my passport and asked me to show up again in a couple of days. During these days, my brother decided to come to Beirut to say goodbye on behalf of my parents, who couldn't travel to Lebanon. When we stood in front of each other face to face, we hugged for the first time since we were little kids. Having him around and eating dinner with him almost every night felt comforting. He was staying at a friend of his because we were worried that Michel, my landlord, might cause trouble if anyone other than Noah slept over at the studio. I wanted to avoid any drama before leaving that shithole.

After a couple of days, I went back to the Swiss embassy to get my visa. At the entrance, the rude Lebanese woman who was always there sized me up and said, "You have been here a couple of days before; I remember you. We didn't miss seeing your face, so what are you doing here?" I politely answered, "I left my passport here a couple of days ago to get my Swiss visa on it." The second she heard "Swiss visa," she looked at me with a wide fake smile and said, "Ah really, so sorry, yes sure, you can go in."

Behind the counter worked an employee other than the one who handled our file; I gave her my name, and she asked me to wait a minute. I was called again to get my passport back with the visa on it. The second I held it in my hand, the amazing employee who managed our case over the past months whispered my name. "Don't go yet; have a seat and wait a little more." I felt nervous. Maybe something went wrong, I thought. After a few minutes, she came back to the counter, asked me to come closer, and said with a gorgeous smile, "I am so happy for you guys. Try not to wait too long to leave Lebanon, okay?" "Can I say something?" "Yes, sure." "You must know you were our angel; we will always remember you. You were the only one who treated us with respect. We will never forget you." "I was only doing my job. What's important now is that you leave as soon as possible to be with Noah."

I left the embassy and immediately called my Noah after sending him a picture of the visa. We wanted nothing but to hug each other for our "Victory." I remember walking back to the studio and feeling so safe just because of the Swiss visa on my passport; I felt protected by this sticker. It was like an armor that shielded me from everything and everyone.

I walked through the same streets I had walked through before every time I went to the embassy or dealt with rocks that blocked my way to be with Noah or to feel safe. I was looking at every corner, imagining they had ears to hear me so I could tell them, "I made it, and it is time to say goodbye." So many parts of me agreed that I don't want to see any of these streets or corners ever again as long as I live.

Before I returned to the studio, I had to stop by Michel's store to tell him I got the visa and was leaving in less than two weeks. This had been the deal between us. He had to be informed two weeks before the end of the month so he could prepare the deposit reimbursement. The same day, Noah booked his return flight, and for me a one-way ticket from Beirut to Switzerland; he wanted to make sure he was with me while leaving Lebanon. He didn't trust the whole system there. They might put obstacles in my way out.

That night, I started packing all my stuff, and I cleaned the studio to make it look brand new and sparkling. When I arrived there six months ago, it was filthy and a hotbed for cockroaches. I was packing and cleaning day and night while being above the clouds out of happiness. I knew there was still looming fear from Beirut airport, but I was determined to endure this last task, no matter what.

The night of my Noah's arrival in Lebanon, I didn't think twice about going to the airport to pick him up. It was about to be the first time seeing and touching him for many months. Seeing him walking toward me in that arrival hall, touching his face, and kissing him in front of everyone made me feel that I could fill the whole Middle East with happiness. My joy heightened even more when Noah met my brother the next day. It was emotional for me to see them together, laughing and making jokes. The day they met, my mom insisted on sending us fresh food with a cab driver, which she had prepared. It arrived in Beirut, still warm.

Eating my mom's cooking with my Noah and my brother meant the whole universe to me. I felt we were all sitting in the same room, my mom, my dad, my siblings, and my Noah, all sharing the same table and food during that dinner. I remember calling my mom on a video-call, and seeing all of us together led us both to break into tears because of how much we longed for each other. Seeing my parents' faces on the phone and hearing their voices around the room talking with us all made me feel that I could smell them; my brain insisted on making the whole thing as real as possible.

Noah and I wanted to say goodbye to the few places we had liked in Beirut. We wanted to let those places see us as the winners and not as the struggling, sad couple living their love in hiding, telling different stories to everyone who started a conversation with us. We had told some people that I was his translator while doing his job in Beirut or that we were old friends. Some others thought we were brothers, but let's be honest here—brothers don't kiss. During these days, I took as many pictures of Noah and me as possible. These last days in Beirut needed to be documented inside our heads, along with these pictures, in case we would get old together and our memories would fail us. On the last night for us in that studio, we decided to open a bottle of wine. We sat all night just drinking and talking like an old couple who had been in love since high school.

Of course, Michel tried to delay the deposit reimbursement as long as he could. He promised to pay it on the morning of the day we were leaving. The day of our flight was all about waiting, waiting to leave that place that ate pieces of me, waiting to be able to show that we are in love publicly, and waiting for Michel to pay what he owed us; Michel ignored my calls the whole day, till he decided to text me that he was busy and would come over later. I could feel and smell that it was the last game he was determined to play with us—he didn't want to pay us a penny back, taking advantage of the whole situation. When I called again in the afternoon, he said rudely, "I will come later. Don't worry, you will get your money, and I need to say goodbye." I didn't believe him for even a part of a second, but I couldn't do anything because, remember, I had no rights at all in that place. I knew he was a piece of dirt who drove a Porsche 911 while owing so much money to people. At the same time, he made Syrian teenagers work for him at the store seven days a week and sixteen hours a day for a pittance. I had overheard that one day, while smoking in the bathroom, in a conversation between two of those Syrian teenagers and a Syrian worker, who called Michel a thief and a scrooge. Michel decided to play power games and showed up less than an hour before our departure. He entered with a big fake smile, hugged me, and acted like the nicest person on earth. He started chatting with us without even mentioning the money. I got a call from my brother, so I went to the balcony to answer him; when I came inside again, Michel was telling Noah that he had been convinced I was lying about the Swiss visa. After all, it was so hard to get one, not only for Syrians but also for Lebanese. While he was talking, he had this sick look in his eyes that said, "I know your secrets; you are fags." Then he said, "I am so sorry, guys, but I couldn't get you the money. The bank didn't let me take a penny. I must wait till the end of the month, so, Noah, can you let me take a picture of your name on the passport so I can transfer the money via Western Union at the end of the month?" My Noah said, "Yes, it is okay. We can wait till the end of the month. We trust you." Noah felt something was wrong, but somehow, he was worried that Michel might harm me at the last moment. The money was never sent to Noah, and Michel always found a way to get rid of us. He used every single play a crook might use from the fraudulent dictionary; he even reached the level of sending us fake pictures of him in the hospital, heavily injured. When he sent these pictures, I told my brother, who was furious about it. He went to Michel's store and saw him having drinks with friends there; my brother wanted to claim the money, but Michel was enough of a mafia guy to the point where he tried to hit my brother with his car and threatened him many times.

When Abu Fadi and my brother came to take us to the airport, it was the second time in my life that I had to leave a place and a country I lived in; that night, I didn't leave a home behind, but a place where I almost shattered into pieces. I turned the lights off and closed the door without even looking back. What I still wanted, I took with me, and what I lost in that place was lost forever. I knew I was about to collect my broken pieces and put them together—this time only in the shape I wanted them to be. We started driving to the airport and left the street and the neighborhood behind. My eyes scanned some corners where I used to talk with Noah on the phone most of the time when I was out. My brain and my soul wanted to preserve some images to remember these times as proof that hope and dreams might, for real, win over reality.

Arriving at the airport brought a mixture of feelings—I was nervous, scared, and happy all together. We stood outside to smoke the last cigarette with my brother and Abu Fadi. Abu Fadi was complaining the whole time that he might get a fine for parking his car in the wrong place, and he wanted to say a quick goodbye and leave while he was my brother's only lift from the airport back to Beirut. My brother wanted to stay until the last second to ensure we would depart safely. Eventually, Abu Fadi left with a hasty farewell and left my brother behind.

Noah and I wanted to be early for check-in, just in

case anything would go wrong, so we might have enough time to solve it. I remember the last time I hugged my brother to say the last goodbye. I walked away from him and looked back every two seconds to let my brain save his features and his smile because I knew I would be in front of only two options in that airport. The first was to be able to fly to Switzerland with my Noah, and the second was that I might be kicked out of Lebanon and back to Syria and be drafted into military service right away.

We sat on a bench in front of the airline's office until check-in was open, listening to a song by the legendary singer Fairouz called "To Beirut." In this song, Fairouz starts singing, "To Beirut, from my heart, I send greetings to Beirut." I always loved this song and all the magic in it. Still, at that moment, I couldn't stand even hearing her angelic voice. I felt like that city didn't deserve even an inch of love from me; as a matter of fact, I always felt that Beirut itself hated me and did nothing but torture me in all sorts of ways. With all the feelings above, I only wished that

Beirut would just let me go.

When the check-in desk opened, we were the first in line waiting there. We could cut the tension with a knife, but we had our tickets, and the Swiss visa was on my passport. When we reached the counter, two employees stood there; the second we handed one of them our passports, they focused only on mine. First, they started whispering with each other until one of them looked at me with a sardonic face and asked in Arabic, "Where's your return ticket?" I answered him politely in English so Noah could understand every word. "Why do I need a return ticket?" He said in Arabic, "Of course, you need one. Who are you to go to Switzerland and stay there, so you should have a return ticket. You are a Syrian, so I can't let you go on the plane." I answered him back in English: "I have a family reunion visa, issued by the Swiss embassy in Lebanon, so I don't need to have a return ticket."

He opened my passport. The other employee stood right next to him, and both were staring inside my passport like morons—checking the Swiss visa, scratching the corners of it with their nails from every side. Noah and I stood there scared, stiff—shocked by what they were doing. Noah immediately showed them the letter from the Swiss immigration authority. Then one of the employees looked at me and asked, "Your visa is a family reunion visa, so who are you going to?" I declared, "I am going to join my family." Then he pointed to Noah. "So, who is he?" "He is Noah." "And who's Noah to you? Who is he?"

They were trying to interrogate us and pushing us to admit that we were a gay couple. My heart raced, and I repeatedly answered, "He is Noah, and I am flying with him tonight to join my family in Switzerland." They were playing the role of the police behind that desk or acting like the Swiss immigration itself, while they had no right to ask me any of these questions as long as I had my Swiss visa and the plane ticket. One of the employees picked up the phone to talk with someone for around five minutes. At some point and after consulting maybe everyone in that airport, he said, "Anyway, you are free to go on the plane, even if I am not sure how and why."

While checking the weight of our luggage, it turned out we had around ten kilograms extra, so they wanted us to pay 300 dollars, a robbery happening in our faces. They refused to get paid except with cash, which made it evident that this money was going into their pockets. Noah had to go to the ATM to get cash, and while I was waiting for him beside the counter, they were whispering and looking disgusted at me the whole time. When Noah, the Swiss, came back with the money, they transitioned into the sweetest mode with him, wishing for a safe, comfortable flight.

The next circle of hell was passport control. There, we had to face the biggest fear. We stood in line, wishing we would get someone friendly and understanding or someone who had enough coffee before coming to the airport to do his job. Noah had to go through passport control for tourists, but he still wanted to wait in line with me. When it was my turn, I remember looking into Noah's eyes quickly before taking a deep breath and walking toward the officer. Before even greeting him, I felt Noah standing behind me like an army, ready to face anything. His look told me: "Everything is going to be fine." At that moment, I knew I would handle everything—no matter what, and nothing could steal my dreams from me. I turned my head toward the officer and handed him over my passport.

Of course, his face changed immediately when he became aware of the navy blue Syrian passport. He checked my document and said, "We gave you only eight days to be in Lebanon; instead, you stayed forever." "Can I say something? To tell you why?" He looked at my passport again, "Shut the fuck up; I don't want to hear anything that comes out of your damn mouth. I don't want to hear your ugly voice at all." He went silent—just scribbling on a piece of paper. While he was writing, I felt my brain was the only thing alive in my exhausted mass of flesh. I could only think of the possibility that he would not let me board the plane with Noah. I just wanted to tell him that I was fooled by a Lebanese person who took money to sponsor me but never did it. I seemed somehow calm, but deep inside, I was going through a fight against falling into a coma.

When the passport control officer finished writing, he gave me the paper and said, "Listen to me carefully. You walk back, and there's an office in the corner of the hall called the airport security office; you give the employee this paper, and when they finish with it, you come through me again. Don't you dare to go through another officer, or I will make them keep you for a few days here, and you will miss your flight."

I did exactly what he wanted me to do and swallowed my pride. We went to that office, where a female officer watched "The Simpsons" on her computer, almost falling into a slumber out of boredom. She took the paper from me and walked into another room. I couldn't stop myself from asking again, "Can I say something?" A part of me was refusing to look anything but a decent person. Annoyed, she asked me,

"What is it?" Another part of me wanted no conflicts or discussions, the part that wanted nothing but to fly out of that pathetic place with Noah. I remember staring at the ground and saying, "Nothing, nothing, forget about it." She stayed inside that room for less than two minutes. We had no clue what exactly they were doing. No one even bothered to explain. After getting the piece of paper back, I returned to the same passport control officer who had ordered me to go through his booth. When my turn came, I stood there without saying even one word, waiting for him to tell me what exactly his plan was. He took a red stamp, marked my passport with it, and said, "You are forbidden to enter Lebanon for one year. You better not mess with it because if you will, we will ban you from entering Lebanon forever." I glanced at him and said, "Do whatever you think fit."

The moment I left his counter behind, I felt the skin of my back cracking from the inside; I felt like two enormous wings were forcing their way out of it to spread to carry me far away. I remember looking back to find my Noah. There wouldn't be any need for my wings or to go anywhere without him. I wished I could hug him or kiss him in front of everyone, but of course, that would have been the worst idea ever in that place. As we walked together to the gate, happiness was lighting our faces. But we knew we were not over yet, and boarding the plane was the last barrier we had to crush.

When our flight was ready for boarding, two grim men in uniforms stood on the sides of the gate checking people's passports and tickets. It was a standard procedure before any flight, but my fear of men in uniforms and authorities, especially in a corrupted place, didn't make me feel safe at all. I was looking at them, repeating my mantra, "It will be fine, it will be fine." That's precisely what happened; everything went fine. They only checked my ticket and passport like everybody else's.

When we took our seats, we were still nervous that anything might go wrong at the last second; I remember the time between the closing of the gate and the take-off of our plane. I couldn't wait to hug Noah and kiss him in front of every passenger on that plane. Everyone who saw me was staring at us with disgust. That didn't stop me. I wanted to tease them. Every time they checked us, I hugged or kissed my Noah. We both were exhausted and needed to take some rest. But I couldn't. I felt I shouldn't even blink and lose a single image of that victory. We were literally flying, just flying away from all the bad memories we had witnessed, lived, and survived.

When I was a boy, we visited a farm my parents' friends owned. On this farm, they caught birds alive in a ruthless way. The farmers used to mix thick jam with some bird's food. The jam, which served as glue, would make the bird's feet stick to it until one of the countrymen would come to catch and collect the birds. On that visit, I remember strolling around with my dad's friend while collecting all the birds alive; we arrived at a tree he had marked to remember the spot of his trap. But there was no bird stuck there. Instead, there was a part of a bird. It was from a bird that had refused to be enslaved, a bird that chose to get rid of a part of his own body, the part that had helped to capture him, a bird that decided to get rid of one of his feet and its claws to save himself. He had focused only on the fact that he had wings and could survive only with them. This is what Beirut meant for me: the sticky jam, and the bird was simply me. I was the bird that sometimes forgot that he owned his wings, but lucky me, I had someone who always reminded me of them when I forgot how powerful they could be. Beirut grabbed a piece of me, a piece that I could keep on living without, but in the end, Beirut grabbed something from me that was not her right to grab because not everything that was taken was given. This is how I felt overlooking Beirut from my airplane window, where I could whisper farewell to some of my claws and to a part of who I had been. I was not even blinking, looking down at that city disappearing behind the slender clouds.

With the final glimpse of that city, I had to ask myself,

"Do I hate Beirut?" and the answer was, "Not at all." I always believed that hate builds nothing and instead causes damage around and inside of us; hate was never a language I learned to speak—it simply had some phonetics that neither my throat nor my soul could even pronounce. So, no, I didn't hate Beirut or the people who turned my life into a living hell there, but to respect any of them, I might need another lifetime in order to do that.

I didn't close my eyes for a second during that three-and-a-half-hour flight to Zurich. I sat on the window looking at the infinity for a while and at my Noah for another. I was repeating the same conversation with myself—that I was on the plane with Noah, that it was for real and not some powerfully imagined story I used to tell myself to fall asleep. Noah woke up every ten minutes to check on me and ask if I was doing okay. As a matter of fact, I was doing great and couldn't believe it. This is why I answered him every ten minutes with an ear-to-ear smile. My Noah was still nervous about what could happen when we arrived at

Zurich airport. I remember him saying it a couple of times in a way that wouldn't scare me or worry, but he said, "It is not over yet, baby, so we will see what's going to happen." Was I also nervous? Absolutely, I was, but that didn't take even a whit out of me feeling safe. I had what you can call trust in Switzerland even before meeting her. I remember flying above an ocean of clouds right before sunrise. The clouds looked like swimming flames, creating one of the most breathtaking views I had ever seen. At that moment, the pilot announced that we entered the Swiss airspace. I started fidgeting in my seat while clapping my hands like a child who knows nothing in the world but happiness. I remember the first time I saw the Swiss Alps. They seemed like majestic gods dressed all in white, except for some holy green accessories on their sides, pieces of jewelry only a god or a goddess could wear.

The first glimpse of Zurich was powerful enough to put a spell on me, the spell that made me say right away: "This is my home; this is where I want to live, grow old, and pass away. This is the place on earth where I will always be happy and safe." I remember falling in love with an old, picturesque bridge I saw between the clouds spanning over a river. The pilot announced being ready for landing at the place I will always call "Home sweet home."

Before we disembarked, I remember asking Noah if he felt okay, and he answered, "We will see, baby, we will see." Noah being nervous made me nervous, too, but something inside me refused to feel anything but safe and happy. When we entered the airport building, I was not even looking around me; I just needed to hold my Noah's hand in public for the first time and walk together without trying to hide our love and relationship. We didn't talk—our hands holding each other were doing that job in their own way; they held the promise that everything would be fine from now on. I recall the moment we arrived at the border control. After Noah took my passport, we walked together toward the counter, where a young blonde officer was working that early morning. My Noah greeted her and handed her his passport next to mine. She looked at him astonished, checking back and forth between my passport and me. Noah said, "This is my boyfriend, and he is here so we can get married." I will remember her face and voice as long as I live, what she said, and how she said it.

Twenty-Two.

What she had said and how she had said it acted like a potent pain killer. She cocked her head while looking at me with a sparkle in her eyes and said only three words: "Welcome to Switzerland." And this is exactly how my love affair with Switzerland officially started, with respect and a welcoming kindness. I was craving some kindness, I was craving some respect, and I was craving the feeling of being treated like a human being again. That was where the birth of my new dream took place: the dream of being Swiss one day so I could feel every second of my life proud to be a part of this land

and its people and try to do my best to make them proud of me.

Noah and I left that airport feeling beyond what people call happiness. We stood in the cold crisp air, smoked a cigarette, and asked each other, "Is it real? Did we really make it?"

We took a cab, and while driving toward downtown Zurich, all I could feel was that maybe I knew this place from a previous life. I felt at home right away. The cab arrived at Noah's neighborhood and parked in front of his building. The driver lifted our luggage out of the trunk, and while putting it down, its wheels broke from the weight and shattered in every direction. The driver apologized sincerely, but I could only think of saying, "Please stop apologizing, and don't worry about it. This is a great sign; it means I arrived here and am not going away anymore." I remember climbing the stairs and breaking the good news to myself, saying, "These are the stairs leading me home." When Noah opened the apartment door, I felt like I had lived there since Noah and I got together. That day, I fell into a deep sleep for the first time in more than ten years; I slept for the first time feeling safe, and nothing on earth could harm me or hurt me again. I was overpowered by a dreamless sleep. My dreams were happening while I was awake.

My Swiss visa was valid for six months, and we had to complete the official registration of our partnership during this period. We went to the city hall the first working day after I arrived in Switzerland. The Zurich civil registry office offered us the possibility of choosing a date in case we wanted to have a celebration or a ceremony. Noah and I would have loved to throw a huge celebration, but it was not an option for us due to our financial situation. We decided to do our own thing the week after, with just the two of us dressed up and having a bottle of wine on the shore of Lake Zurich after finishing all the procedures in the city hall. When we set the date, I realized again that I had no one to be there on this important day: no family, no friends, no one I even knew. What gave me comfort was that my best friend, partner, and first and last love would be by my side from now on— all the time.

The date we had chosen was 4/ 4. Noah wore a suit and tie and looked like the most handsome man on earth. I had my suit and a bow tie I had bought once in Syria. We arrived at the city hall and were asked to sit and wait in front of a desk. We were both nervous, holding each other's hands. The employee was upset, trying doggedly to restart the computer. There was a technical problem. She started hitting the screen and telling Noah in Swiss German how annoyed she was. I couldn't understand a word she was saying. I feared something was about to go wrong. Eventually, the computer started working normally, and she immediately apologized in English for her behavior.

After she had prepared the official certificate of our partnership to sign, Noah handed it over to me with an adorable smile to go first. I held the pen to write my signature, and in a second, I was drawn back to the time when I had to invent my signature for the first time in my life while being arrested in Syria. For a moment, I had the same state of mind and the same anxiety I had in that moment in the past. Going through this during that unique event forced me to close my eyes for a second so I could scream inside at all these bad memories and shout at them to leave me alone. I remember what I was telling myself while putting my signature on that paper: "Here's the only memory I should keep about my signature; I am signing to be with the love of my life."

I gave the pen to my Noah, and while he was signing, I could hear the clicks of a camera. Someone was taking pictures. A man stood armed with a camera and a long lens, taking pictures of us. I was still traumatized by Lebanon, and ten seconds before, I had to suppress flashbacks from dark memories in my life, so I grew anxious right away. I remember putting my head behind Noah's back, trying to hide. I was literally freaking out and started whispering to Noah, asking him to make the camera guy stop. Noah looked at the door and said, "What? Who? What do you mean pictures of us?" Then he laughed, "He is taking pictures of us because this is the photographer of our newspaper. I think my boss sent him." When we finished the papers, the employee congratulated us and handed us the pen as an official gift from the city.

While leaving that office, I was simply in shock and didn't know how to react. Noah asked the photographer, "Who asked you to come here?" He grinned, "You will see in a bit." I remember walking downstairs while the photographer didn't stop taking pictures of us.

We walked toward that big, beautiful, old wooden door. We didn't know what to expect. When the door opened, we saw Noah's boss smiling and holding two red roses in her hand. The second we took the steps down to the forecourt, we were amazed to see some of Noah's friends and colleagues forming a guard of honor, throwing flowers and candies. My soul was smiling even before my lips, seeing all these strangers showing us all that love, being that happy for us. Looking at the pictures from that day, I feel a mix of happiness and sadness. They show me how skinny and broken I was, but ready to recover all over again. Noah's boss had insisted on planning something beautiful for us on our special day. She brought two tables and placed them in front of the city hall, filled glasses with champagne and drinks. Noah and I were in the center of that beautiful scenery while the photographer was taking pictures of us kissing with the impressive church in the background, releasing balloons into the sky. Strangers were passing by, watching a gay couple getting married, and some congratulated us with genuine smiles on their faces. Kids watched us like they would watch any ordinary wedding. They would come and ask for some candies. I couldn't stop drinking, trying to process everything that was happening, everything that sounded and looked like heaven in my eyes. I insisted on holding the "Just got married" balloon, so someone tied the rope to my arm, and I paraded it through the old town of Zurich.

We roamed through the alleys until we stopped at the old bridge I had seen from the plane. I had to pay my respects to that city and its river. I was admiring the marvelous view with the lights of the old town reflected in the gentle water. Seeing this beauty made my whole past turn into a rolling film reel, and arriving at that specific scene, time just stopped. I wanted time to stop there and to relive this moment over and over again. The peace, beauty, love, and appreciation were Zurich's only colors and fragrances that night. Have you ever heard of someone living inside of a perfume vial? Well, you just did.

***

Epilogue

They say, "You might know my name, but not my story." At this point, some of you learned both my name and many of my stories; for others, now you know my story but not my name. Learning people's stories makes them way more real to our eyes. Their stories brought them to be who they truly are today. I was able to expose myself to you all. I stripped, and I am not sure if my name would make any difference. In front of you, I took off the layers of fear, of being weak, of being sad, scared, disappointed, hurt, stabbed, cheated on, and betrayed. Above all, what made me indeed survive everything on my own was, beneath it all, the true me— the one who wanted nothing but to be seen as how I see myself and who I truly am.

I got married when I was twenty-six years old. Still, my soul was many decades older. That day was one of the lights of my life, even though I wished my family was with me or any of my friends if I had any left. But this is how life is. Nothing is perfect, and as a matter of fact, perfect is boring. Perfect happens only at the end of Hollywood movies, but trust me on this: happy endings might happen to any of us. The most important things are to work on the relationship with yourself constantly, stay in love with yourself, learn to know when and where to put yourself first, and never give up, as maybe you were pushing hills long before you knew you could. Sometimes, we might be blinded by the pain and can't see clearly anymore; just be patient and remember that help could be pretty close by—from outside or even from within.

I also learned that our feelings are there somehow for one reason or another, and they don't randomly exist in us. Fear is there when we need to be scared of something, and only by experiencing it can we learn the fact that we are strong and brave. Hate is there so love can flourish on the other side, and it is up to us to choose on which weighing pan we want to stand. Anger is there because we need to be angry sometimes, and we should embrace it; it is okay to be angry at something or someone as a way of enabling these feelings to stop hurting you. No one is asking you to forgive and forget—it's all up to you, and as I always said, "I'm not a saint to forgive, nor do I have Alzheimer's to forget." Forgiveness would give you the peace you deserve, no doubt. It is okay to feel lonely, and it is up to you if it will push you to have unhealthy friendships or relationships or if it will make you become creative and reveal some of your talents. It is okay if you are bullied. Pain offers you a chance never to become one, especially to yourself. You would learn how much you love and respect yourself, so you will act to protect this awareness and fight back when needed. And if you ever think of ending your life—always remember, my dear, you might start this shit all over again—somewhere that it might be even worse. Who learned to stand up always after falling; if they stood long enough, they could learn to fly.

You must understand another thing about charming, kind, and loving people. Their other side is just as extreme; the hell they survived made them gentle, so don't ever take their self-control for weakness. The

beast inside is sleeping—not dead. The writer and poet
Ghibran Khalil Ghibran said: I learned the silence
from the babbler, the indulgence and forgiveness from
the fanatic, and the kindness from the wicked and the
mean; the strangest thing about all the above is that we
do not acknowledge the credit of these teachers.

***

ABOUT THE AUTHOR

Lucian S. was born in Syria in the 1990s.

STRIPPED: A MEMOIR is his first published book. He writes under a pseudonym. He has been living and working in Zurich, Switzerland, since 2018.

www.luciantheauthor.weebly.com